THE BOUNDARYLESS GOD

How God's Wall-Breaking Love Transforms a Divided World

BY
STEPHEN FUKA FEKA

STEPHEN FUKA FEKA

Copyright © 2025 by Stephen Feka Fuka

All rights reserved. No part of this publication may be reproduced, distributed, or transmitted in any form or by any means, including photocopying, recording, or other electronic or mechanical methods, without the prior written permission of the publisher, except in the case of brief quotations embodied in critical reviews and certain other noncommercial uses permitted by copyright law.

Paperback

ISBN: 978-1-918039-55-9

Good Reach *Publishing*

Dedication

To all who are quietly unravelling
To those who feel disqualified by their failures
and trapped behind walls—
within and without.
May you discover the God who is already on your side,
wrecking ball in hand.

FOREWORD

A Reflection on Boundaryless Love

When I first encountered *The Boundaryless God*, I found myself pausing often to reflect and to breathe. Each page opened a window into the vast tenderness of God, inviting me to listen anew to Love's unguarded heartbeat. This is a book to peruse gradually and to pray with. It reveals the God who crosses every border we draw, who meets us not at the edge of perfection, but in the trembling spaces where our strength ends and grace begins.

In his unique style, Father Feka writes from a space of sacredness, from the dust of human struggle and the radiant light of divine compassion. The stories, rooted in the soil of Congo, Cameroon, and the shared realities of our world, unveil a Love that refuses containment. It is the love that dismantles our fortresses of pride and fear, tears down the walls of false security, and builds in their place the open sanctuary of mercy. In these pages, holiness is not distant; it is disarming. God's touch is gentle and transformative.

Reading *The Boundaryless God* felt like standing before a horizon newly cleared of fog and seeing, at last, how divine love stretches far beyond our inherited boundaries. It calls us to a tenderness fierce enough to heal division and to a faith brave enough to let love lead us where certainty cannot.

May this work awaken something quite yet courageous within you.

May it draw you ever closer to the God whose love knows no bounds, and whose mercy always finds a way through.

Angèle Nkamsi MSHR

Angèle Nkamsi

Dublin Ireland

TABLE OF CONTENTS

INTRODUCTION 1
PART I: RECEIVE THE WRECKING BALL 4
   Chapter 1 God's Love Is a Demolition Crew 6
   Chapter 2 The God Who Breaks His Own Rules 15
   Reflections On The Dust, The Silence, And The New Eyes 25
PART II: SEE THE INVISIBLE FENCES 28
   Chapter 3 The Algorithmic Pharisees 30
   Chapter 4 The Pandemic Paradox 42
   Chapter 5 The Sacred Cows We Keep 53
   Reflection On The Burden And The Blessing Of Seeing 67
PART III: PRACTICE HOLY TRESPASS 70
   Chapter 6 The Art Of Holy Trespass 72
   Chapter 7 The Currency of Curiosity 86
   Chapter 8 The Counter-Physics of the Kingdom 100
   Chapter 9 The Terrible Freedom of Forgiveness 114
   Chapter 10 When Hospitality Hurts 130
   Reflection On The Blessed Bruising And The Work Ahead 144
PART IV: BUILD BROKEN PIECES 147
   Chapter 11 Beauty in the Cracks 148
   Chapter 12 The God Who Enters the Wound 160
   Chapter 13 From Echo Chamber to Sanctuary 174
   Chapter 14 The Last Enemy is a Mirror 188
Epilogue: The Demolition Continues 202
Bibliography 204

INTRODUCTION

Let's be honest — this book is not for people who have everything together. It's not for the spiritually triumphant, the morally confident, or the emotionally polished. It's for those of us who are quietly unravelling inside well-ordered lives. For the pastors who preach grace but no longer feel it. For the caregivers who are running on fumes but can't admit it. For the high-functioning faithful who know how to smile through holy exhaustion — and are terrified that someone might notice the cracks.

If that's you, you're not weak. You're waking up.

This chapter isn't a theology lesson. It's a reckoning. It's about what happens when your carefully constructed identity — your spiritual success, your calling, your sense of control — shatters. When the image of yourself as "the strong one" finally collapses under its own weight. And it's here, in that collapse, that the fundamental transformation begins, not with a fresh revelation or a second wind, but with ruin.

I know, because I've lived it. This is the story of the night I hit bottom in a mission chapel in the Congolese rainforest. But more than that — it's the story of what God did next. The story of a love so wild and uninvited that it didn't come to decorate my life; it came to wreck it — for the sake of saving it.

If you've ever feared that your failure disqualifies you from God's love, this chapter is for you. If you've been clinging to your spiritual performance like armour, I invite you to lay it down. Because before God can rebuild something true, he will lovingly tear down everything false.

Let the wrecking begin.

Take a look at the life you've built. It's a carefully constructed thing. Each year of your career is a new brick. Each success is a fresh coat of paint. Your social media feed is the manicured lawn, trimmed and curated to show only the best angles. We are all architects of our own image, living under the immense pressure of a world that rewards

Strength and penalises cracks. We are taught to build higher, reinforce the separation, and project an image of perfect, impenetrable stability. We protect ourselves from failure, from judgment, from shame.

But what if the deepest, most dangerous walls aren't the ones facing the world, but the ones we've built inside our own hearts? The quiet, hidden walls of pride that tell us we can handle it all on our own. The cold, damp walls of shame that insist we are too broken to be loved. We spend our lives decorating the outside of these inner prisons, hoping no one — not even God — gets a look at the mess inside.

This is why, when we finally ask God for help, we often have a particular request. We're looking for a decorator, not a demolition expert. We want a God who will hang a new picture on our wall, maybe fill a few cracks, or give us a beautifully wrapped gift to place on our mantelpiece. We expect God's love to be a polite guest — one that admires our construction and doesn't dare rearrange the furniture.

This was the God I thought I knew. For years, I believed my job was to build my life for him, to present a fortress of faith that was strong and respectable. Then, in a single, devastating moment, my fortress crumbled to dust. And in the rubble of my most profound shame, I made a shocking discovery: God's love didn't arrive with a decorative ribbon. It came with the thunderous, terrifying, and ultimately healing force of a wrecking ball.

The two chapters in this first section are about this discovery. They are an invitation to stop building and to start embracing a divine love that is not neat or conditional, but relentlessly invasive and restorative. Before we can build bridges to others, we must first allow God's love to demolish the walls of shame and pride within us.

It's time to welcome the wrecking ball.

PART I:
RECEIVE THE WRECKING BALL

We spend so much of our lives building. We construct identities brick by brick, polish the surfaces of our successes, and carefully curate the image we present to the world. We are taught that strength lies in solid walls and impenetrable defences. I certainly believed this. For years, my priesthood felt like the careful construction of a fortress – a place of certainty, competence, and control. I thought my job was to build something respectable for God.

Then came the night in the Congo – the night my carefully built fortress crumbled into dust under the weight of my own fear and failure. In that ruin, I discovered a truth I had never been taught: God's love doesn't always arrive as a comforting gift to decorate our lives. Sometimes, necessarily, it comes as a wrecking ball. Before we can ever hope to build bridges out into the divided world, we must first allow God to demolish the hidden walls we've built within – the walls of pride that tell us we are self-sufficient, and the walls of shame that whisper we are unworthy.

The two chapters in this first part explore this terrifying, liberating truth. They invite us to stop reinforcing our defences and instead welcome a divine love that is not polite or predictable, but relentlessly invasive and ultimately restorative. It is the necessary first step – the painful, holy demolition that clears the ground for grace. It is time to welcome the wrecking ball.

Chapter 1
God's Love Is a Demolition Crew

Let's be honest — this book isn't for people who have it all together. It's not for the spiritually triumphant, the morally confident, or the emotionally polished. It's for those of us who are quietly coming undone beneath well-ordered lives. For the pastors who preach grace but no longer feel it in their bones. For the caregivers who are running on fumes yet can't bring themselves to stop. For the high-functioning faithful who have mastered the art of smiling through holy exhaustion — and live in quiet fear that someone might glimpse the cracks. If that's you, you're not weak. You're finally waking up.

This chapter isn't a theology lesson — it's a reckoning. It's about what happens when your carefully constructed identity — your spiritual success, your calling, your control — collapses like glass under pressure. When the image of yourself as "the strong one" finally gives way to truth. And it's here, in that breaking, that fundamental transformation begins. Not with a fresh revelation or a burst of inspiration — but with ruin.

I know, because I've lived it. This is the story of the night I hit bottom in a mission chapel in the Congolese rainforest. But more than that — it's the story of what God did next. The story of a love so wild and uninvited that it didn't come to beautify my life; it came to wreck it — so it could be rebuilt.

If you've ever feared that your failure disqualifies you from God's love, this chapter is for you. If you've been clinging to your spiritual performance like armour, I invite you to lay it down. Because before God can rebuild something true, He must first tear apart everything false — gently, but thoroughly.

Let the wrecking begin.

A small brick mission church stands in a remote Congolese village; its silhouette etched against a slate-grey sky. On this night, storm clouds smother the moonlight and warm rain falls in torrents, drumming on the tin roof and turning red earth to mud. Inside the chapel's mud-brick walls, shadows leap to the rhythm of lightning as thunder rattles the crucifix on the altar. The air is thick and feverish — smelling of damp earth and burnt wax. In this church — my church — on this night, I would face the deepest unravelling of my life, the moment when everything within me finally broke.

It was well past midnight when I heard the frantic pounding on my rectory door. I opened it to find a young man from the distant village of Bikoyo, drenched and trembling. Rainwater streamed down his face as he gasped, "Father, please come — Jean is dying!" Little Jean was a nine-year-old boy, the son of a local catechist. My stomach dropped as I recalled his shy smile just a week before. Now his brother stood before me, eyes wide with terror and fragile hope.

For a moment, I froze. My heart slammed against my ribs. Every instinct screamed to go — yet a flicker of fear took hold. The roads were perilous, and the threat of bandits or rebel militias that prowled after dark was all too real. Only a year earlier, armed rebels had attacked a seminary in the north, forcing seventy-seven seminarians to flee for their lives. That memory — and every horror story I'd ever heard — flashed before me.

"He's been convulsing with fever all day," the boy cried over the rain. "Please, if you don't come now, he won't last until morning!"

Go, urged my conscience. Yet another voice whispered: *If you go, you may never return.* Shame rose in my throat. I knew that as a priest and shepherd, I should not think of myself — and yet I did. I looked at the black, slashing rain — and hesitated.

"I'll… I'll leave at first light," I finally said, the words tasting of ash and fear. I watched the desperate hope fade from the boy's eyes, replaced by a dull despair. He nodded silently and disappeared into the rain. I closed the door, my chest tightening with self-loathing. *God, what have I done?*

When dawn broke through the storm's remains, I sped towards Bikoyo on my battered motorcycle. The road had turned to swamp, but I pressed on, praying that the boy would hold on. When I arrived, the village was wrapped in an unnatural hush. The wailing began before I even reached Jean's family hut. His mother emerged, clutching a small, lifeless bundle. Her cry — raw and unearthly — was the most sorrowful sound I have ever heard. I knew I was too late.

I sank to my knees in the mud as the mother collapsed into my arms, rocking her son's body. All I could do was whisper, "I'm here... I'm here now," knowing that now was a mercy too late.

That night, back at the chapel, I hit rock bottom. I locked the door and fell to my knees before the altar, staring up at the crucifix. Every ounce of composure I had worn like

Armour disintegrated. A strangled cry tore from my chest as I pounded the altar. "I failed him! I failed that little boy... and I've failed You!"

I remembered my ordination day — lying prostrate, vowing to be a shepherd who would lay down his life for his flock. And here I was, prostrate again — but this time in defeat. When the moment came, I hesitated. I'd feared death, and a child had died instead. I ripped the white collar from my neck; it felt like a costume for a fraud. Lying on the cold stone floor, I felt a hollowness so vast it seemed my very faith had been drained from me. This was it — the bottom of everything.

We often imagine God's love as a reward for strength. It isn't. It's His response to our brokenness. In the Christian tradition, the word is *agape* — not sentimental affection, nor a transactional love earned by merit. *Agape* is a relentless, pursuing, unconditional love that runs toward us not when we're polished and perfect, but when we're knee-deep in the mud of our own undoing.

The ancient Hebrews had another word for it: chesed. A love born of covenant — of loyalty that never gives up. *Chesed* says, "Even if you are faithless, I will remain faithful." It's the love that stays when every rational voice says to walk away.

I didn't understand that on that night. Lying on the floor, I saw only failure. I believed I had sinned myself beyond God's reach. But the collapse of my inner walls — my pride, my self-reliance, my fear — wasn't punishment. It was mercy in its fiercest form: God's love as a wrecking ball. My fortress of self-worth had to crumble because it was built on illusion. Only through its ruin could something true be built — not on my strength, but on the bedrock of grace that grows strongest in our shame.

I stayed on that chapel floor until the first blush of dawn. Exhausted, hoarse, aching — I felt years older. As I rose, cassock streaked with mud, I knew that if I were to stand again, it would have to be as a different man.

That was the night I truly learned what it means to be broken. The night, Grace sent its demolition crew.

I used to think the great enemies of faith were out there — doubt, sin, the world. But now I know the most dangerous enemy hides within: the quiet wall we build when we believe God's love is only for the worthy.

That night, I learned otherwise. Divine love doesn't stop at the border of our shame — it shatters it open.

But what happens when the walls God wants to destroy aren't just internal? What if the barriers are sacred, institutional — even scriptural?

What happens when God begins to dismantle not only your pride, but your very religion?

That's where we go next.

FIELD GUIDE:
CHAPTER 1 INTEGRATION

The work of welcoming the wrecking ball is not a one-time event; it is a daily practice of surrender. Use these tools this week to move the truth of this chapter from your head to your heart.

1. Theological Meditation Point

Carry this single, powerful truth with you this week. Write it on a note card or set it as a reminder on your phone. Let it reframe how you see your relationship with God.

God's love is not a reward for my strength, but a response to my brokenness. It does not arrive to decorate my fortress; it comes to demolish it.

2. Questions for Reader Practice

Set aside a few minutes to reflect on these questions in a journal or in quiet thought. Be honest with yourself. There are no correct answers, only honest ones.

- In what area of your life are you currently asking God to be a 'decorator'—to neaten up the surface or fill over a few cracks—when he might be inviting you to welcome the 'demolition crew'?

- Reflect on a past moment of failure or shame. In what ways did you, as I did on that chapel floor, feel you had sinned yourself 'outside the reach of God's grace'? How does the concept of chesed—a loyal love that stays even when we are faithless—speak to that memory now?
- The chapter defines God's love as 'relentlessly invasive and restorative'. Which of those two words — 'invasive' or 'restorative'—do you find more challenging to accept in your life right now, and why?

3. Mini-Guide for Daily Embodying: The Wrecking Ball Mantra

This is a small, embodied practice to help you begin the act of surrender.

Step 1: Identify One Wall. In this moment, name one inner wall you are actively defending. Is it a wall of pride ("I can handle this on my own; I don't need help")? Or is it a wall of shame ("I am too broken to be loved; if they knew the real me, they would leave")?

Step 2: Practise the Mantra. At least once a day for the next three days, find a quiet moment. Place a hand over your heart, take one deep breath, and whisper this mantra aloud:

"God, I welcome your love not as a decoration, but as a demolition crew. I surrender this wall to you."

Notice what it feels like in your body to say those words. This small act will begin to train your heart for the deeper work of the Agape Lab that follows.

AGAPE LAB #1: Womb-Breathing Prayer

The feeling of shame makes us want to curl up, to hide, to make ourselves small. It is a feeling of utter exposure. The antidote is to experience, in our own bodies, a sense of being unconditionally held and accepted. This simple, embodied practice is designed to help you internalise the *agape* love of God, especially in moments when you feel unworthy. We call it *"womb-breathing"* because it simulates the perfect safety and acceptance of a child in the womb, held and nourished before it has done anything to *"earn"* it.

Chapter 2
The God Who Breaks His Own Rules

When your walls have crumbled, and the dust has settled, the temptation is to start building again — new rules, more precise lines, safer categories. After all, chaos is terrifying. We reach for structure, for control, for clarity. But here's the uncomfortable truth: even holiness can become a hiding place.

After the wrecking ball comes the reckoning.

This chapter is for those trying to rebuild their faith after a collapse — for the ones stepping over the ruins of certainty, still desperate for something solid. But what if God's next move is even more disorienting? What if He begins to dismantle not just your inner pride, but your sacred assumptions? What if, just when you start to rebuild, He breaks His own rules to show you what love actually looks like?

We, humans, are brilliant at creating rules. We build systems of belief, codes of conduct, and social contracts to bring order to chaos. In our churches, our companies, our families, and our nations, we draw lines — lines that decide who belongs and who doesn't, what is acceptable and what is not. These rules promise safety, clarity, and identity. They become the tall moral thresholds we guard, protecting the perimeter of our righteousness.

There is nothing inherently wrong with rules; they can be healthy and life-giving. But a subtle danger lurks. Over time, we can fall in love with the boundaries themselves. We begin to worship the rules more than the God who inspired them. The system designed to protect life starts to suffocate it. Holiness — a word meant to describe God's vibrant and loving nature — becomes a synonym for separation and exclusion. We become so focused on defending the boundary that we fail to see the wounded soul bleeding on the other side of it.

But what if God's primary business isn't gatekeeping? What if his holiest act is breaking through our sacred boundaries for the sake of a single lost person?

To understand the boundary-breaking nature of God, I had to look at Jesus. And we must look honestly. We often sanitise Him, turning Him into a tame figure who never offended anyone. Yet the Gospels tell another story. Jesus was constantly in trouble for breaking the most sacred social and religious rules of His day.

Consider His encounter with the Syrophoenician woman in the Gospel of Mark. She was a Gentile — an outsider to the "chosen" circle. When she begged Jesus to heal her daughter, He initially rebuffed her with a harsh, rule-bound statement: "It is not right to take the children's bread and toss it to the dogs."

That was the sacred rule. The boundary was clear: the mission was divine, but the scope was humanly defined. Yet the woman, driven by desperate love for her child, broke a rule of her own. She answered with a stunning humility and wit: "Lord, even the dogs under the table eat the children's crumbs."

In that instant, the rule gave way to a relationship. Jesus saw her faith — and the boundary dissolved. He healed her daughter.

This was not an isolated moment; it was a pattern. Think of His scandalous habit of dining with sinners. In that culture, sharing a meal wasn't casual; it was a declaration of intimacy and kinship. When the Pharisees — the rule-keepers of their age — saw Jesus eating with tax collectors and prostitutes, they were scandalised. "Why does your teacher eat with such scum?" they demanded. To them, holiness meant distance. But Jesus saw it differently.

He made a radical theological statement with bread and wine: God's welcome is not a reward for the righteous, but a feast for the outcast. He stepped beyond the gates of separation to enact a more ancient and powerful law — the law of grace.

"It is impossible to become truly human if we only love those whom our systems have taught us to love. To follow Christ is to cross every border we once built in His name."

— *James Cone, The Cross and the Lynching Tree*

That same collision between sacred rule and human suffering plays out today. Consider the story of a pastor I know — Reverend Emmanuel Mbarga.

Reverend Mbarga was the kind of preacher people both respected and feared. His church, Ebenezer Tabernacle, stood at the edge of a Cameroonian township — a fortress of stone and stained glass. Inside, the pews were straight-backed and unforgiving, much like his sermons on moral decay. In his world, God was Holy. And holy meant separate.

But it wasn't a lightning bolt that changed him. It was a boy.

A young man named Elie, who used to sit quietly in the back row, had once been the subject of one of Emmanuel's fiery sermons about "unnatural desires."

The next day, Elie's mother came to the church. Elie had taken his own life. The note he left ended with:

"I tried. I swear I tried to pray it away."

When the door closed behind her, something inside Emmanuel broke. He sat alone in the sanctuary for hours, staring at the empty seat where Elie had sat. For the first time in years, he wept, whispering to God,

"Is this what you wanted? Is this what I've become?"

The following Sunday, Emmanuel stepped into the pulpit.

"I have to tell you something," he said, his voice trembling. "I preached about what God hates. But I didn't preach about mercy — or what God weeps for."

Gasps rippled through the pews.

"A young man from our church, Elie… he died by suicide last week. And I believe — I know — that part of his pain came from here. From me."

A silence heavy as grief settled over the room.

"I thought I was defending God's truth. But in my zeal, I forgot His heart. And I am sorry."

Some people stood and walked out, their heels echoing like gongs of disapproval. But others stayed. After the service, an old woman cupped his face in her hands and whispered, "Now, you are our pastor."

The church changed. The pews thinned at first, but new faces appeared — people who had once been too afraid to enter. They came for honesty. Emmanuel no longer preached to be right; he preached to heal.

Reverend Mbarga's story is more than a personal confession — it's a mirror held up to us all—every institution — religious or secular — risks becoming its own Ebenezer Tabernacle. We build policies, doctrines, and cultural norms to guard integrity. But when protecting the institution outweighs protecting the people it serves, those lines turn into walls. Elie became a casualty of a system that prized doctrinal purity over a young man's life.

The tragedy is that it still happens — quietly, daily — in churches, schools, and workplaces, whenever our unspoken rules tell someone they are not welcome, not worthy, not safe.

The stain of that moment never left Emmanuel. But it became what he later called "holy scar tissue." A scar is a place where the skin has grown back stronger. His public apology — the act of tearing down his own authority — was his demolition. It stripped away his doctrinal armour, leaving him exposed before his congregation.

It reminded me of my own night on the chapel floor — when pride and fear had to die before something new could live. This is the terrible, beautiful secret of faith: God cannot work through a fortress, but He can do wonders with the rubble.

Emmanuel's ministry became powerful not despite his failure, but because of it. He discovered that a pastor's most sacred duty is not to be right, but to make space — a home for those who have been told they don't belong anywhere else.

His sermons no longer ended in fire and brimstone. They ended in a whisper:

"Come home. Just as you are."

"When love stretches itself beyond the borders of law, it does not destroy the law — it transfigures it."

— *St Gregory of Nyssa, Homilies on the Beatitudes*

Emmanuel's story doesn't just invite us to tear down fences — it forces us to face the invisible ones we still defend. In our digital world, the walls are no longer built of stone; they're coded, curated, fed to us by algorithms that know our fears better than we do.

Before we can love across these new divides, we must first learn to see them.

That's where we turn next.

FIELD GUIDE:
CHAPTER 2 INTEGRATION

Having welcomed the demolition of our inner fortresses, we now turn our attention to the fences we build to keep others out. This week, use these tools to begin the courageous work of examining your own rules.

1. Theological Meditation Point

Carry this challenging truth with you. Let it be a filter through which you view your interactions and firmly held positions.

My most sacred rules are only holy if they lead to more love. If a rule I am defending causes another person to feel unseen, unsafe, or unworthy, I may be defending my own certainty, but I have forgotten the heart of God.

2. Questions for Reader Practice

Set aside a few minutes for honest reflection. This is not about shaming yourself for having rules, but about prayerfully examining their proper function in your life.

- Reverend Mbarga's unspoken rule was that *"the church must not compromise."* What is one of your own unwritten, *"sacred"* rules for your life, faith, or family? Where did this rule come from?

- Reflecting on the rule you just identified, can you think of a specific time when defending it caused you to prioritise being *"right"* over being in a loving relationship with someone?
- The chapter highlights how Jesus consistently broke religious and social rules to include people like the Syrophoenician woman and to eat with those considered *"sinners."* What group of people today do your personal or communal *"fences"* tend to keep at a distance?

3. Mini-Guide for Daily Embodying: The Fence Finder

This is a simple practice of awareness. The goal is not to change your rules overnight, but to simply see them for what they are. This is a crucial first step before the deeper work of "The Reverse Examen."

• **Step 1**: Notice Your Judgements. For the next three days, carry a small notebook or use a notes app on your phone. Your only task is to gently notice and write down the moments when you feel a strong, rule-based judgment towards another person. Examples might sound like: *"A good parent wouldn't do that," "They shouldn't dress that way for church,"* or *"That's not a very Christian thing to say."*

• **Step 2**: Just Write, Don't Act. Do not act on the judgement or shame yourself for having it. The act of noticing is the entire practice. At the end of the three days, review your list and, for each item, ask the question Reverend Mbarga was forced to confront: "In defending this rule, have I forgotten God's heart?"

AGAPE LAB #2: The Reverse Examen

Many of us are familiar with the traditional Examen — a prayer of reviewing our day to see where God was present. The Reverse Examen is a tool for looking at the other side: identifying the *"holy rules"* in our lives that are actually walls against love. These are the righteous-sounding principles we use to keep people at a distance. Reverend Mbarga's rule was *"The church must not compromise."* It sounded holy, but it became a wall that cost a young man his life. This lab is a guided reflection to help you courageously identify your own sacred fences, so that, like him, you can begin to dismantle them for the sake of love.

Reflections On The Dust, The Silence, And The New Eyes

Let us pause here for a moment — in the quiet stillness between two movements. If you have journeyed with us through the stories of Part I, you have stood on holy and perhaps painful ground. You have felt the tremor of the wrecking ball within your own soul. You have knelt on the cold chapel floor in the heart of the Congo, tasting the dust of loss and failure. You have felt the weight of a pastor's public apology — and the terrifying vulnerability that follows when the fortress of our certainty finally crumbles.

The end of a demolition is not triumphant. It is quiet. It is the hush that follows the crash — the air heavy with the dust of what used to be. We are left standing in the rubble of our own pride and fear, exposed and stripped of familiar defences. The temptation in that moment is to rebuild — to raise the same walls once more, perhaps a little taller, a little safer. But what if the purpose of demolition is not merely to clear the ground, but to clear our vision? What if the silence itself is an invitation — to see differently, to see truly?

For it is only then that sight begins. For years, we live inside the fortresses of our own making, peering out at the world through narrow arrow-slit windows. We imagine we are seeing reality as it is, when in truth we are only seeing it through the distorted glass of our own defences. We see threats that justify our fears. We see enemies that excuse our walls. We see a world that seems as cold and unyielding as the stone we ourselves have laid.

The demolition of that inner fortress is disorienting — but it is also the beginning of sight. When we no longer need our walls to protect the ego, when we no longer rely on certainty to feel safe, the window itself disappears. The dust settles, and we find ourselves standing in an open field — the horizon vast and startlingly clear. We realise the grime we thought stained the world was in fact on our own glass. And this clarity — this fresh, unfiltered seeing — is the hidden gift of collapse.

This kind of sight is what Scripture calls discernment. It is the gift of the Spirit — the ability to see the world not as we are, but as God is. We glimpse it in Jesus, who could always see the person behind the label — the woman behind the word *adulterer*, the human heart beneath the title, *tax collector*. The religious leaders of his day, the Pharisees, could not see this; their vision was blocked by the towering fortresses of their righteousness and their carefully built systems of purity. It was only when their self-reliance shattered — when the disciples huddled, defeated, behind locked doors — that their eyes were opened to recognise the risen Christ for who he truly was.

To have our inner walls demolished is to be given new eyes. Eyes that see beyond threat and caricature. Eyes unclouded by the need to be right. Eyes that can discern the quieter, more insidious fences criss-crossing the world around us — the ones we once ignored because we were too busy defending our own.

And that is where our journey now turns. Armed with these clearer eyes, we are called to become spiritual diagnosticians — to read the landscape of our lives, our digital worlds, our communities, and our beloved yet broken institutions, and to name the invisible fences we once mistook for the natural order of things.

Part II of this book is a field guide for this new way of seeing. It is an invitation to take the sight forged in the rubble of your own heart and turn it outward — toward the divided world God loves so fiercely.

The demolition is over. Now is the time to see what the light reveals.

PART II:
SEE THE INVISIBLE FENCES

Allowing the wrecking ball of God's love into the private fortress of our hearts is the first — and most terrifying — step. If you have walked through the dust and rubble of that demolition, you already know its power and its cost. But the work does not end there. In truth, it has only just begun.

When God tears down our inner walls of shame and pride, He gives us something in return: new sight. Eyes that see beyond self-interest. Eyes that perceive the world not as a catalogue of threats to be managed, but as a fractured landscape filled with people He loves. With these new eyes, we begin to notice what we once missed. We start to recognise other fortresses — not the ones we built ourselves, but the ones we inhabit every day, often without even realising they exist. They are the subtle, insidious, and frequently invisible fences that quietly divide our world.

In the twentieth century, walls were made of concrete and crowned with barbed wire. We could see them, touch them, protest them. Today, the most formidable walls are unseen. They are not built from stone, but from data. They rise with every click, every "like," every algorithm engineered to keep us comfortable within our tribe and suspicious — even furious — toward everyone else. These are the fences of the twenty-first century.

They are the digital walls of social media echo chambers, which reward outrage and punish nuance. They are the ideological walls of political polarisation, which turn neighbours into caricatures. They are even the theological fortresses that twist healthy boundaries into fear-based barriers, blocking the free flow of grace. These fences promise safety, but deliver isolation. They do not simply mirror division — they multiply it.

The chapters ahead are a field guide for discernment — for learning to see what has long been hidden. Before we can cross these fences, we must first train our eyes to recognise them for what they are. Our journey now turns outward — from the rubble within our souls to the fractured landscape of our world.

And it begins with the most powerful fence of all: the one in your pocket.

Chapter 3
The Algorithmic Pharisees

After my own fortress of pride was shattered on that chapel floor, I was left standing amid the ruins of my certainty and the echo of my undoing. The first invisible fence I had to confront was the one I had built in my own mind. I had confused theological precision with faithfulness, mistaking rigid categories of right and wrong for the heart of God Himself. Before I could recognise the walls dividing the world, I first had to face the algorithm of my own righteousness — that quiet internal code which filtered out nuance and rewarded my own biases.

Anjali's story — set in a world of hashtags and dopamine hits — may seem a world away from my mission chapel. Yet, her awakening to a curated, algorithmic reality was a journey I was only beginning to understand myself.

Every generation has its temples. For the Pharisees, it was the synagogue. For Anjali, it was Twitter. The liturgy had changed — likes instead of lambs, hashtags instead of hymns — but the impulse was ancient: build a fence around the truth, guard it with zeal, and cast out the impure. And what better way to cleanse a world than with fire — one tweet at a time?

Every morning, Anjali rose at 6:15 a.m. in her Delhi apartment — a two-room flat near Lajpat Nagar with a balcony overrun by basil and bougainvillea. Before brushing her teeth, before chai, she opened Twitter. Within seconds came the hit — dopamine disguised as justice. Another Dalit boy was beaten for drinking from a public tap. A viral image of riot police dragging a hijab-wearing student through a university courtyard. A thread titled, "Why your *silence is violence*."

This was her world — and her work. At twenty-seven, Anjali was a rising voice in India's social justice movement, running workshops on caste sensitivity, coordinating legal aid for protesters, and writing op-eds for major online platforms. Her Instagram stories were heat-seeking missiles, exposing privilege and naming oppressors with the righteous fury of someone utterly convinced she stood on the right side of history. Rage was her currency, and the algorithm rewarded her fire, amplifying her words through networks of academics, activists, and celebrities. With each like and share, her certainty hardened.

That certainty seeped into life offline. Her mother, a devout and gentle woman, hated it.

"You used to be such a happy child, beta," her mother would say, her voice laced with sorrow, Anjali could hardly bear. "Now you're always angry."

"Maybe you should be angry too, Ma," Anjali would reply, cold and sharp. "You light incense for Lakshmi while Dalit children clean your drain. Doesn't that bother you?"

"I never hurt anyone," her mother whispered, eyes brimming. "You talk like I'm the villain."

"Silence is violence, Ma." The words were a clean, righteous wall — a verdict disguised as virtue.

This instinct to build barriers in the name of righteousness is nothing new. It is ancient — perfected two thousand years ago by the group Jesus most often clashed with: the Pharisees. We use Pharisee today as shorthand for hypocrite, but their role was more complex. They were not villains in their own eyes — they were guardians of holiness in a corrupt world. Their mission: to keep the community pure by building a geder le-Torah — a fence around the Law.

This fence was made of hundreds of extra rules designed to stop people from even approaching sin. Noble in theory — fatal in practice. Over time, the fence became more important than the people it was meant to protect. It evolved into a spiritual algorithm — a feedback loop for the virtuous — filtering out messy, complicated souls in favour of a curated version of faith.

Anjali, too, had built her fortress. Her hashtags — #SmashCaste, #ResistHindutva — were the bricks. Her call-outs were the scaffolding. And her golden rule — "Silence is violence" — was the barbed wire on top. It was an efficient system for excluding nuance, especially among those she loved most. "Zeal without wisdom is fire without light."

— Saint Isaac the Syrian

Jesus reserved His harshest critiques for such fences. When the Pharisees rebuked His disciples for skipping ritual handwashing, He accused them of "abandoning the command of God to hold to human tradition." He then exposed their hypocrisy: they had invented a rule called Corban, a religious loophole that allowed a man to dedicate his property

To God so it couldn't be used to care for his parents. They had built a sacred justification for breaking one of God's most sacred laws of love. They had made their ideology more important than their mother.

Jesus called it what it was: a sickness of the soul. The worship of the fence.

Anjali's carefully constructed fence was about to fall. It happened at 2:38 a.m., under the blue glare of her phone, in the heat of the Karnataka hijab protests. She stumbled upon a viral photo — a Muslim student, wide-eyed and surrounded by saffron-scarved boys shouting "Jai Shri Ram." It was the perfect image — the pure narrative of victim and oppressor. She quote-tweeted it with, "This is what fascism looks like," and watched it explode: 12,000 likes in an hour.

She felt righteous, purposeful — seen. Until, hours later, someone replied with a longer, unedited video.

She watched. Paused. Replayed.

The boys were shouting, yes — but they hadn't cornered her. Security had stepped in seconds later. The image she'd shared had been cropped, zoomed, and framed to tell a cleaner, angrier story. The room seemed to hum; her chest tightened.

I didn't lie, she told herself. I just didn't ask questions.

Her tweet was still surging. The outrage machine was still running. But now, she could see the architecture beneath it — the timeline that always told her one story. The cousin she'd unfollowed for posting a festival photo. The echo chamber that had become her faith.

A memory flickered: her father singing off-key bhajans on the way home from temple, buying her roasted peanuts from a street cart. She had long buried that image as a relic of oppression — but now it resurfaced, achingly human.

The next morning, she deleted the tweet. No explanation. Then came the silence — the ache of withdrawal. Her fingers twitched toward retweets, craving the hit of righteousness.

But another voice rose within her:

Is this truth — or is it performance?

That question changed everything.

Anjali broke her own algorithm. She followed a conservative Dalit journalist who criticised liberal tokenism. A Hindu priest posting only about sanitation projects. A Muslim feminist who called out hypocrisy in every camp. Her feed became a battlefield of contradictions — messy, disorienting, alive.

"The truth does not belong to a camp. It lives at the threshold where certainties tremble."

— *Simone Weil*

Her posts grew quieter, her tone more measured. "Starting to realise that calling people upper-caste trash might dehumanise the very people we're trying to reach," she wrote. She lost 600 followers overnight.

The backlash came swiftly.

"You've changed." "Wow, so now you're gaslighting survivors?" "Centring oppressors now?"

She didn't reply. The old Anjali would have fought back. The new Anjali simply read — and grieved. Then she opened her Signal app, found the cousin she had unfollowed, and typed:

"Hey. Want to grab coffee sometime? I think I owe you a conversation."

There was no reply. Not yet.

Anjali's reckoning wasn't just personal — it was a collision with one of the most powerful systems shaping our world. Her mind and the algorithm were dancing in perfect, destructive sync.

Neuroscientists call it confirmation bias — the brain's craving for reinforcement. Social media didn't invent it; it industrialised it. Every like triggers dopamine. Every click taught the machine what to feed her next. Outrage meant engagement. Engagement meant profit. Her attention was not the product — it was the currency. "The algorithm doesn't care what you believe — only how long you stare." — Tristan Harris.

What Anjali endured was a modern dark night of the soul — the moment she realised that certainty masquerading as faith was simply a well-designed echo chamber. Her act of intentionally "polluting" her feed was a form of repentance — a spiritual rebellion. It was

A declaration that truth matters more than tribe, and people more than platforms. It was the bravery to be lonely for the sake of love.

This is the first act of freedom: recognising that the most advanced surveillance system on earth is aimed not at our homes, but at our hearts — mapping our fears, monetising our vanity, and building prisons with our consent. Breaking free is not a digital detox. It is spiritual warfare.

But what of those who never wake up? What happens when the algorithm wins?

To see the cost, we need only look at Anjali's brother, Rohit.

Once a bright boy who dreamed of being a pilot, he now ran a conspiracy blog from his childhood bedroom. His descent began slowly, then with frightening speed. During the lonely months of the pandemic, he stumbled into anti-vaccine Telegram groups, then deeper into nationalist echo chambers, Great Reset videos, and QAnon-inspired forums. He started speaking a new dialect of paranoia: secret plots, holy wars, spiritual conspiracies.

His parents laughed at first. Then they argued. Then they wept.

At a family wedding, the fracture turned visible. Rohit refused to sit beside a Muslim family friend. "They are agents of cultural jihad," he said flatly. Anjali screamed; he screamed louder. Their father — a gentle man who only ever wanted peace — collapsed from the strain.

They haven't spoken since.

Sometimes, late at night, Anjali scrolls through Rohit's old Facebook page, back before the anger — before the memes and madness. She stops at a photo: the two of them as children. She's grinning in pigtails, and he's wearing her bangles, laughing. Before the hashtags. Before the fences.

Rohit's story is tragic, but far from rare. Millions now live inside what scholars call epistemic bubbles — sealed echo chambers, reinforced by invisible code. They're not just reading different facts; they're breathing different realities. And behind many of these bubbles lies the same dark intelligence — political, economic, ideological — that knows division is the surest weapon.

Rohit wasn't merely misguided. He was a casualty of a new kind of warfare — one fought with code, not guns.

The paths of Anjali and Rohit reveal the defining choice of our age. Both were caught within invisible fences. One, through grace and courage, began to climb out. The other mistook the walls for the world.

Seeing these fences isn't easy. It demands that we question our own righteousness, sit with discomfort, and acknowledge that the monster beyond the wall may be just another frightened human being. It is a daily act of humility — the only road that leads back to connection, back to the messy, complicated, sacred work of loving our actual neighbours.

Anjali's screen had once been a sword. Now, it had become a mirror.

But before she could build again, she had to learn to sit quietly among the ruins of her own certainty.

And in the next chapter, we enter another battleground — where truth, fear, and fortress-thinking collide under the guise of safety.

FIELD GUIDE: CHAPTER 3 INTEGRATION

Breaking free from our digital echo chambers is not a matter of deleting an app; it is a conscious act of spiritual warfare. Use these tools to begin the work of reclaiming your attention and your heart from the forces that seek to divide.

1. Theological Meditation Point

Carry this truth with you as you navigate your digital world this week. Let it transform your scrolling from a passive habit into a mindful practice.

My social media feed is not a neutral window onto the world; it is a curated reality designed to monetise my outrage. Every click, like, and share is an act of spiritual formation — either building a wall of certainty or a bridge of curiosity.

2. Questions for Reader Practice

Set aside time to reflect on your own digital life. Be ruthlessly honest, but also compassionate with yourself. The goal is awareness, not shame.

- Anjali's online life was fuelled by the "dopamine hit" of righteous rage. What is the primary emotion your social media feed elicits in you on a typical day? Is it anger, fear, envy, connection, or something else?

- The Pharisees built a "fence around the Law" to separate the "clean" from the "unclean." Who has your algorithm taught you to see as "unclean," irredeemable, or as an enemy? How has it flattened them into a caricature?
- Anjali's cold certainty created a wall between her and her mother. Have your online convictions — or the tone you use to express them — created distance or pain in any of your real-world relationships?

3. Mini-Guide for Daily Embodying: The Curiosity Click

This is a small, concrete practice to begin intentionally breaking your algorithm, just as Anjali did. This is the first step towards the deeper work of Algorithmic Sanctification.

Step 1: Find a Different Story. The next three times you are on social media, consciously resist the urge to click on a story that generates immediate anger or easy agreement. Instead, find one post from a source or person you respectfully disagree with but consider thoughtful (like Anjali following the conservative journalist she found).

•**Step 2**: Ask the Question. Before you read the article or watch the video, pause and ask yourself Anjali's powerful question: "Is this truth, or is it performance?" Then, engage with the content with the single goal of understanding the other person's perspective, not rebutting it. You do not have to comment or react. The entire practice is to gently expose your heart and mind to a story the algorithm would never show you.

AGAPE LAB #3: Algorithmic Sanctification

The word "sanctification" means "to set apart for holy use." Our digital feeds are, by default, set apart for commercial use — to capture our attention and sell it. This lab is a spiritual practice designed to reclaim that space.

It is a conscious, weekly habit of curating your digital world not for outrage or comfort, but for curiosity, empathy, and a fuller picture of the truth. It is the practical toolkit for the journey Anjali started.

This exercise will guide you through a step-by-step process of auditing your feeds, intentionally following voices that challenge you, and developing new online habits that build bridges instead of deepening trenches. You will learn to transform your feed from a high-walled fortress into holy ground for seeing the humanity in others.

Chapter 4
The Pandemic Paradox

When Good Boundaries Become Bad Barriers

Do you remember the silence?

In the first weeks of the global pandemic, the world went still. The roar of traffic faded, the skies emptied of planes, and the familiar rhythms of life came to a sudden, screeching halt. In that eerie quiet, a single, urgent question echoed through every household, every heart: How do we stay safe?

That question turned us all into architects of distance — cartographers of caution. We learned new words like *"social distancing"* and *"lockdown."* We drew circles of safety around our families, our homes, our very bodies. We began, quite literally, to build boundaries.

But the crisis forced a deeper question — one that sits at the heart of faith itself: What is the difference between a boundary that protects and a barrier that imprisons? When does self-preservation turn sour, hardening into self-righteous isolation?

The pandemic didn't invent this paradox; it only magnified it, holding a mirror to the hidden architecture of our hearts. It revealed that some of us instinctively build gates, and others, hedges.

This tension runs through Scripture itself. On one hand, there is the wisdom of Proverbs — a call to guard our hearts with care. On the other hand, there are Jesus's parables — warnings against the damnation of exclusion and pride.

Proverbs tells us: *"Above all else, guard your heart, for everything you do flows from it."* A call to discernment, not defence — to godly boundaries, not walls of fear.

The Hebrew word for "guard," natsar (נָצַר), does not mean to barricade oneself within a fortress. It suggests careful cultivation — like a vinedresser tending his vineyard. He

Builds a fence not to isolate the vines but to protect them from what devours — the boars, the thieves, the blight. He keeps out the rot, but lets in the sun and rain. A godly boundary is a gate, not a prison bar — open to what nourishes, closed to what poisons.

During the pandemic, this looked like learning to honour our limits: stepping back from the endless doom-scroll of anxiety, walking away from toxic online arguments, and preserving quiet corners for prayer and rest. It was the wisdom of knowing what to let in — and what to keep out.

Yet there is another, darker impulse we must confront. It's the story of the older brother in Jesus's Parable of the Prodigal Son — the man who did everything "right." He stayed, obeyed, performed, and took pride in never rebelling. His life was a monument to duty.

But when grace walked back through the gate — in the form of his broken, dirt-stained brother — the elder son refused to enter the celebration.

Scripture says plainly: "He became angry and refused to go in." When his father came out to plead with him, bitterness spilled out like poison: *"All these years I've been slaving for you and never disobeyed your orders. Yet you never even gave me a young goat to celebrate with my friends."*

His worth was tethered to performance; his righteousness was measured by comparison. His boundary had hardened into a wall. His sense of duty, severed from mercy, had become his prison.

The feast was open to him — the music and joy were his to share — but he chose the cold comfort of self-righteousness over the warmth of his father's embrace.

The pandemic exposed both instincts within us: the desire to build wise gates that protect, and the temptation to erect rigid barriers that judge — walls so strong they lock even us out of grace.

In a mid-rise apartment complex on the outskirts of Nairobi — The Emerald Towers — those thresholds hardened. The complex was affluent, its gates guarded, run by a committee of retired professionals with an obsession for order.

As the news worsened, fear seeped through the spotless corridors. The homeowners' board acted fast, drafting a set of "safety" rules designed to turn the compound into a fortress.

No one entered or left except verified residents. Delivery drivers, even those carrying essential medicine, were banned from entry. Domestic staff — housekeepers, nannies, caretakers — were suspended indefinitely, regardless of circumstance. The rules were absolute, airtight, unquestioned.

Among the residents was Mwikali, a single mother working exhausting night shifts as a nurse at the nearby hospital. When she asked for an exemption so her neighbour could watch her children while she worked, the chairman replied curtly:

"It's nothing personal, Mwikali. We just can't take the risk."

His tone made it clear: her crisis was unfortunate, but acceptable collateral for their "safety."

Then came the breaking point.

One evening, Mr Omari, a 76-year-old widower in Unit 3B, suffered a mild stroke. He collapsed on the floor, unable to reach his phone — its battery long dead. His cleaner, who used to check on him twice a week, was barred from the compound.

He lay there for fifteen agonising hours — trapped, unseen, inside the "safe" walls of his apartment. A neighbour, noticing his curtains unmoved, finally raised the alarm.

When paramedics broke in, they found him dehydrated, weak, and furious.

"They caged me in like a criminal," he muttered as they lifted him onto the stretcher.

Days later, the board shrugged off blame.

"We followed the rules," they said.

But the rules had become a shield against compassion. What began as prudent safety had decayed into architecture built on fear.

The Emerald Towers became a case study in how fear short-circuits moral reason. Institutions, driven by liability, prioritised the protection of their image over the protection of their people. The goal was no longer care — it was control.

The residents had kept the letter of the law and lost its spirit. Like the elder brother, they were dutiful but detached — faithful to the rulebook, faithless to the heart of God.

Their boundaries, meant for safety, had become barriers to love.

Just a few blocks away, on a quiet street called Kanungu Lane, a different kind of fortress was forming — one made not of iron gates but of grace.

There was no committee here, no formal charter. Just seven households connected by a WhatsApp group and an old-fashioned sense of neighbourliness.

When lockdown came, they made a radical decision: they would not retreat.

They called, they planned, they acted. They created a rota for grocery runs, tracked needs on a shared Google Sheet, and organised pharmacy pickups to limit exposure. For their elderly neighbours, they set up "porch visits" — masked, distant conversations that preserved both safety and connection.

They even pooled funds to provide masks and sanitiser to a nearby informal settlement, recognising that their safety depended on their neighbours.

Then came the test.

Mama Achieng, a 92-year-old widow with severe asthma, fell ill. Her caregiver had just tested positive and was quarantined. Under the rules of The Emerald Towers, she would have been abandoned.

But Kanungu Lane saw her differently. They didn't see a liability; they saw their shared responsibility.

Two young women, both vaccinated, volunteered to form a "care pod." Wearing donated protective gear, they delivered meals, medicine, and comfort — never reckless, but never absent.

On the sixth day, a voice note appeared in the group chat — trembling but clear:

"You people... you are God's hands. You remind me we are not alone, even now."

No law was broken. No boundary is ignored. But love had found its way through the gate.

"Duty without mercy is cruelty in disguise."

— Cornel West

Kanungu Lane embodied what sociologists call mutual aid — communities taking direct responsibility for one another instead of waiting for distant systems. Agile, compassionate, and grounded in trust, they showed that care is not chaos; it's courage.

The pandemic stripped us bare. It showed what we build when the world collapses. Some, like the residents of The Emerald Towers, built bunkers. Some built corridors of control and called it safety. And some — like the families on Kanungu Lane — built bridges of grace.

Scripture does not call us to recklessness. But it never blesses cruelty in the name of purity. The heart of God has gates — not to keep people out, but to let grace flow through.

And so, the question remains:

Will our boundaries serve fear, or love?

Will they guard the heart — or harden it?

Before we argue about who's allowed in, we must ask a harder question:

What kind of house are we building? Fortress or feast? Gate or wall?

The next chapter walks into the sacred spaces where that question becomes even more uncomfortable — when the "holy" itself becomes untouchable.

FIELD GUIDE:
CHAPTER 4 INTEGRATION

The pandemic may be receding, but the practice of building walls in the name of safety is a timeless human impulse. Use these tools this week to examine the spiritual architecture of your own heart and the boundaries you maintain.

1. Theological Meditation Point

Carry this simple but profound distinction with you. Use it as a lens to evaluate the *"rules"* you live by.

A godly boundary is a gate, built from love to protect my soul for the sake of others. A fear-based barrier is a wall built from pride and fear to protect my comfort at the expense of others.

2. Questions for Reader Practice

Set aside time for honest reflection on the boundaries in your own life. The goal is not to eliminate all boundaries, but to ensure they are serving the right purpose.

- Think of a specific boundary you are currently maintaining in a relationship, at work, or in your community. Is it functioning more like a discerning "gate" that lets in nourishment (like on Kanungu Lane) or a rigid "wall" that enforces isolation (like at The Emerald Towers)?

- What is the primary emotion driving the boundary you just identified? Is it a love for health and true flourishing, or is it fear, anxiety, or a need to control the outcome?

- The older brother's sense of duty and fairness became a wall that locked him out of his own father's celebration. In what area of your life might your own commitment to being *"right"* or *"responsible"* be preventing you from experiencing or extending grace?

3. Mini-Guide for Daily Embodying: The Gatekeeper's Question

Before the deeper work of the "Love-Leap Litmus Test," this small practice will help you build the muscle of discernment in your daily decisions.

Step 1: Identify a "No." Sometime this week, you will inevitably need to set a boundary by saying "no" to a request, an invitation, or an opportunity. Identify one of these moments.

Step 2: Ask the Question. Before you give your answer, pause for a moment. Take a single breath and ask yourself this simple Gatekeeper's Question: Is the "no" I am about to give serving love, or is it serving fear?

There may not be a simple answer, and the "no" may still be the right one. The entire practice is the act of asking the question itself. It begins to train your heart to distinguish between a gate that guards and a wall that wounds.

AGAPE LAB #4: The Love-Leap Litmus Test

How can you tell the difference between a healthy boundary and a fear-based barrier in your own life? This lab is a practical tool — a *"litmus test"*— to help you discern the nature of the walls and gates you maintain.

It consists of a series of diagnostic questions that you can apply to any boundary in your life, whether it's in a relationship, at work, or in your community. By honestly answering questions like, *"Does this boundary create more connection or more isolation?"* and "Is this protecting my soul or just my comfort?" you can begin to see which of your boundaries are life-giving *"gates"* that need tending, and which are life-draining *"walls"* that God might be inviting you to tear down.

Chapter 5
The Sacred Cows We Keep

Confronting Walls In Our Institutions

It doesn't start with malice. Sacred cows are born in the warmth of good intentions — fed by memory, clothed in reverence, raised by those who simply want to preserve what once felt holy. But in every generation, there comes a moment when those sacred cows stand in the doorway of justice, blocking the path with gentle smiles and quiet rules.

This is the story of what happens when love for the past begins to strangle the future.

Every sacred cow was once a calf we loved too much to question.

In every faith, there comes a moment when reverence hardens into resistance — when what began as devotion becomes defiance against renewal. This chapter begins at that threshold: where the altar of faith is guarded not by angels, but by fear masquerading as fidelity.

Margo Barnes had been a fixture at Pine Hill Community Church for over thirty years. She taught Sunday school, led the prayer chain, and her sweet-potato casserole was the undisputed champion of every church potluck. Her love for Pine Hill was etched into the landscape of her life; her father had laid the first stone of the original chapel. The church wasn't just a building — it was heritage, heartbeat, home.

But lately, a dull ache had begun to stir — a quiet unease that rose whenever she thought of her granddaughter, Ellie. Bright, funny, full of life, Ellie had recently come out as gay and had asked a simple, devastating question over the phone:

"Grandma, if I visited your church, would I be welcome?"

Margo had paused for a heartbeat too long.

"Well, of course you would, honey… but," she'd added, the words tasting hollow, "we don't really talk about that kind of thing here."

What she didn't say — what she couldn't — was that Pine Hill operated under a "quiet exclusion" policy. It was invisible but absolute. No hateful sermons, no open condemnation — just polite, well-mannered distance. Couples like Ellie and her partner could not serve in leadership, could not become members, and were gently, systematically discouraged from attending at all.

This was the church Margo loved with her whole heart — and she was suddenly terrified it might break her granddaughter's.

This is the danger of our most beloved institutions: they rarely collapse from attack; they calcify from within. Tradition becomes policy. Unity becomes avoidance. And before anyone notices, a sacred cow is born — an idol of politeness, self-preservation, and fear of controversy — standing squarely where the disruptive love of God should move freely.

"The Church is always tempted to turn from a place of radical welcome into a museum of the pure." — Father Greg Boyle.

We see this pattern most clearly in the story of the one institution meant to be God's living heart — the Temple in Jerusalem. As Pope Francis reminds us, our structures must serve people, not the other way around.

The Temple was meant to be a meeting place between God and humanity, but by the time of Jesus, it had become something else entirely. Under layers of commerce, legality, and control, it turned into a marketplace of exclusion.

When Jesus entered and overturned the tables of the money-changers, it wasn't, as Pope Francis says, a "violent outburst." It was holy grief made visible.

On the surface, the money-changers provided a useful service: exchanging pagan Roman coins for Temple currency, so worshippers could pay their taxes and buy sacrificial animals. Logical, practical — even necessary.

But in practice, it had become a pay-to-pray system. The poor were overcharged. The Gentile court — the only space outsiders could worship — was choked with commerce and noise. Worship had been fenced off, blocked behind financial, ethnic, and ritual walls that God had never built.

When Jesus overturned those tables, He was not simply clearing clutter; He was dismantling an invisible wall that had become the architecture of exclusion. His anger was not temper — it was grief.

Quoting Isaiah, His voice thundered through the silence:

"My house shall be called a house of prayer for all nations, but you have made it a den of robbers."

Jesus wasn't rebelling against worship — He was reclaiming it. He didn't destroy the Temple; He set it free. He flipped the tables, not out of rage, but to make room for the forgotten to come home.

Margo Barnes knew deep in her bones that a table needed flipping at Pine Hill. She also knew a quiet, sixty-three-year-old grandmother could not do it with force.

The sacred cow at Pine Hill was simple: Don't rock the boat.

The board — kind, godly men she had known for years — spoke of "unity" and "faithfulness to Scripture," but beneath it she saw fear. Fear of conflict. Fear of loss. Fear of change.

So, her campaign began not with a protest, but with coffee.

One by one, she invited elders to her kitchen table — the same table where their children had once done homework — and told Ellie's story. She asked one, gentle question:

"What would Jesus say if Ellie walked through our doors on Sunday morning?"

In her small group, she began to raise the topic again — carefully, humbly. Not to argue, but to humanise. She reframed the issue from "culture war" to "pastoral care."

During a tense budget meeting, she quietly read the Parable of the Lost Sheep aloud. Then she looked around and asked, softly,

"Have we left any sheep outside the fold because we were afraid of the mess they might bring in?"

The resistance was quiet but sharp. One evening, Tom — an elder and old friend — leaned forward with a troubled look.

"Margo," he said gently, "I think your love for family is blinding you to God's truth. We can't bend Scripture for feelings."

Her hands trembled under the table. The accusation hurt — that love was a weakness. She breathed, prayed, and met his gaze.

"Tom, I'm not asking you to bend Scripture," she said softly. "I'm asking you to remember why it was written — to reveal the heart of a God who leaves the ninety-nine to go after the one."

She cried all the way home.

Then came the breakthrough. With Margo's encouragement, Ellie wrote a letter to the leadership.

"I'm not asking you to change overnight," it read. "I just want to know if people like me can sit in my grandmother's church — to sing, to cry, to pray — not as projects to fix, but as people to love."

The pastor read it aloud at a retreat. Silence fell. Then a younger board member whispered,

"Maybe it's time we stop guarding a gate God never locked."

Three months later, Pine Hill voted to affirm the full inclusion of LGBTQ+ members. The vote was not unanimous — but it was decisive.

That Christmas, Ellie sat beside Margo in their usual pew. During *O Come, All Ye Faithful*, she wept quietly. Margo wrapped her arm around her — and prayed in gratitude for a table finally turned.

Margo's story is more than personal. It's a case study in how love reforms institutions.

Over time, all organisations develop what sociologists call institutional inertia — the tendency to protect what exists rather than pursue what's right. The fear of losing donors, members, or peace becomes more powerful than the mission itself.

Margo's genius was that she didn't attack her church; she reminded it of its heart. Using Scripture, prayer, and relationship, she spoke its native tongue — calling it back to its founding spirit.

Her courage wasn't loud, but it was holy. The quiet courage of a prophet, the grief of Jesus in the Temple. She loved her church enough to refuse its lesser self.

"True religion is not the curation of control, but the unleashing of compassion." — bell hooks.

This dynamic isn't unique to churches. It exists anywhere a mission becomes management.

Devika Patel discovered this at Hands Together, a respected U.S.-based non-profit supporting women's cooperatives in South Asia. Its mission statement gleamed: *"Empowering women through locally driven entrepreneurship."*

But behind the scenes, Devika saw a drift. Fundraising had become king. Projects were chosen for their photogenic appeal, not their genuine need. Field reports were rewritten to fit donor expectations. Impact was measured in likes, not livelihoods.

The sacred cow was the comfort of the donor. The invisible wall was a story too polished to be true.

The crisis came before the annual "Faces of Freedom" gala. The plan: fly three women from Nepal to America, parade them onstage, film their testimonies.

Devika protested.

"They are partners, not props," she said. "We promised we'd never ask them to perform their trauma."

A senior executive replied coolly,

"It's just one night, Devika. We need this campaign to hit seven figures."

The mission had become a stage.

Risking her career, Devika spent two weeks preparing a confidential report for the board — documenting every distortion. It ended with a piercing question:

"Have we become better at telling stories than at changing them?"

"When the narrative becomes more important than the people in it, we are no longer doing justice — we are staging it." — Ada María Isasi-Díaz

Her report caused turmoil — and then transformation. A new committee was formed with field representatives given real authority. The gala format was redesigned to centre local voices without exploitation.

Later, a board member told her,

"Thank you. You reminded us of the difference between good optics and good work."

Devika's story captures what experts call mission drift — when the metrics of survival outweigh the meaning of service. When the story about the work outshines the work itself.

Her courage forced the organisation to confront its own sacred cow — to ask whether it served people or performance.

Sacred cows often begin as necessary structures — rules for unity, systems for stability. But when they become idols — when they demand loyalty instead of offering life — they lose their soul. Jesus overturned tables not to destroy faith, but to restore it.

Margo spoke not to divide her church, but to heal its welcome. Devika challenged not to shame her institution, but to set its compass true.

We all live within institutions we love — imperfect churches, well-meaning charities, legacy workplaces. Love does not mean silence. Sometimes the most faithful love looks like disruption.

If we genuinely believe in a house of prayer for all nations, then we must be willing to clear the way for all to enter — even if it means flipping a few tables.

The question isn't whether our institutions have sacred cows. It's whether we have the courage to face them when they block the door to grace.

Reading Margo's story, I'm reminded of the quiet rules that once governed my own priesthood. The sacred cow I served wasn't pride —

it was fear. Fear of failure. Fear of appearing weak before the flock. That fear made me hesitate on that rainy night in Congo.

The "quiet exclusion" Margo challenged in her church was the same exclusion I practised in my own heart — walling off my weakness from others and from God.

To see the sacred cows in our institutions is deeply personal work, because they often graze in the same pastures as the idols in our own souls.

In the next chapter, I walk into the trauma ward — not of the body, but of the soul — to ask:

What happens when the very sanctuary meant to heal us becomes the place that wounds us most?

FIELD GUIDE:
CHAPTER 5 INTEGRATION

We all inhabit institutions we love — imperfect churches, well-meaning non-profits, and legacy workplaces. Loving them well does not mean silent complicity; sometimes, the most faithful love looks like disruption. Use these tools to cultivate the courage and wisdom to challenge the sacred cows in your own communities.

1. Theological Meditation Point

Carry this truth with you as you navigate your role within the institutions you are part of. Let it redefine what faithful participation looks like.

My love for an institution is best expressed not through silent loyalty, but through the courageous, gentle disruption that calls it back to its true heart and mission.

2. Questions for Reader Practice

Set aside time for a prayerful and honest assessment of the communities you belong to. The goal is not to foster cynicism, but to cultivate a loving and discerning eye.

- Margo's church had the sacred cow of "Don't rock the boat." Devika's non-profit had the sacred cow of "Donor comfort over client dignity." Think of an institution you are part of — your

church, workplace, or community group. What is its unspoken sacred cow?
- Both Margo and Devika risked their social standing and careers to speak up. What is your greatest fear when it comes to challenging a sacred cow in your own community? What do you feel you have to lose?
- Margo's campaign began with coffee and storytelling. Jesus's action in the Temple was a prophetic disruption. Reflecting on your own institution and its particular challenges, which approach — gentle internal advocacy or a more public, prophetic disruption — feels more needed right now, and why?

3. Mini-Guide for Daily Embodying: From Critique to Compassion

Before the deeper analytical work of "The Institutional Examen," this small practice is designed to shift your own heart's posture towards a frustrating institution.

Step 1: Identify an Institution. Name one institution in your life that is currently a source of frustration for you. It could be your workplace, your church, your local school board, or even your government. For one day, simply notice the critical or judgmental thoughts you have about it.

Step 2: Practise a Prayer of Loving Concern. For the next three days, instead of mentally critiquing the institution, take one minute to practise a prayer of loving concern for it. You might use Jesus's prayer for the Temple:

"May this become a house of prayer for all nations."

You might pray for a specific leader within it by name. The goal is to shift your heart from a posture of opposition to a posture of compassionate desire for that institution's true healing and restoration.

AGAPE LAB #5: The Institutional Examen

Just as the traditional Examen helps us reflect on God's presence in our personal lives, the Institutional Examen is a tool for prayerfully assessing the health of the institutions we belong to. It is a private, guided reflection designed to help you identify the "sacred cows," unwritten rules, and invisible palisades that may exist within your church, workplace, or community group.

This lab offers a series of diagnostic questions to help you see your institution with new eyes. Is the mission clear and centred? Who is being unintentionally excluded?

Where has "the way we've always done it" become a barrier to love or justice?

This is not a tool for cynical critique, but a practice of loving discernment — one that equips you to become a gentle, courageous, and healing presence within the communities you care about most.

Reflection On The Burden And The Blessing Of Seeing

If you have journeyed with us through Part II, you can no longer unsee what you have seen. It is like putting on a new pair of glasses — the world that once felt ordinary now reveals itself as a carefully engineered architecture of division.

You now see the code humming beneath the surface of our lives:

- The invisible fences are not made of stone but of data, designed to keep us in a profitable state of outrage.

- The subtle ways that healthy boundaries, born of safety, can curdle into fear-based barriers that isolate and wound.

- The sacred cows grazing quietly in the corridors of our most beloved institutions — the unwritten rules that sanctify exclusion in the name of unity.

To see this hidden architecture is both a gift and a weight. It is a blessing, because seeing the truth is the first step toward freedom. But it is also a burden, because once you have seen it, you can no longer pretend these structures are natural or harmless.

You see the harm they cause. You feel their cold shadow across your family, your workplace, your house of worship.

And so, the question is no longer What do we see? It is What will we do with what we now see?

This burden of vision is a holy burden. It is the beginning of sharing in the grief of God.

I imagine God's heart breaking each time an algorithm turns a neighbour into a caricature — each time a church's policy of "quiet exclusion" makes a beloved child of God feel unwanted.

The ache you may carry after reading these stories — the ache for Anjali's fractured family, for Mr Omari's lonely apartment, for Ellie, who only wanted to know if she could sit in her grandmother's pew — that ache is sacred.

It is the sound of God's heartbeat awakening in your own chest.

This holy grief is not meant to paralyse us; it is meant to propel us. It is the fuel for the journey ahead.

Apathy is the luxury of the blind. But for those who have been given eyes to see, compassionate action becomes the only faithful response.

And yet, the scale of what we see can feel crushing. We glimpse the global reach of disinformation, the stubborn inertia of institutions, the ancient roots of division — and the temptation whispers: It's too big. Too broken. Too late.

But that is a lie.

The fences may be systemic, but the mortar that holds them together is human — made of choices, postures, and relationships. And therefore, the work of demolition begins in the same place: within us.

Systems do not change until the people inside them change. And people are not changed by argument or data, but by the transforming power of human connection.

That is why the only faithful response to seeing a wall is to begin crossing it.

This is the logic of the Incarnation.

God did not shout solutions from the safety of heaven. He trespassed.

He put on flesh and blood, crossed the ultimate boundary between the divine and the human, and walked among us — entering our messy, fractured world not as an observer, but as a companion.

PART III:
PRACTICE HOLY TRESPASS

You now have new eyes.

If you've journeyed with us this far, you can see the invisible fences everywhere — in your social media feeds, in your community's unspoken rules, perhaps even within your own family. You see the quiet architecture of division. But seeing is not enough.

To see a wall and choose not to cross it is simply to build another one within yourself.

The call of a boundaryless God is not merely a call to perceive — it is a call to move.

And this may be the most frightening part of the journey. It asks us to leave the safety of our own territory, to step across a line into someone else's world. It demands that we risk rejection, misunderstanding, and discomfort — the sacred costs of genuine connection.

This is the practice of Holy Trespass — the art of intentionally and lovingly crossing the man-made divides of politics, religion, and culture for the sake of relationship. It is the radical belief that the person on the other side of the wall is more real, more sacred, than the wall itself.

The chapters that follow are not just reflections — they are invitations. They offer postures, practices, and stories meant to equip you for this holy — and deeply necessary — act of trespass.

Chapter 6
The Art Of Holy Trespass

Becoming Boundary-Dissolvers

Some walls are built with brick. Others are built with silence, fear, and the quiet conviction that certain people are beyond reach.

But every so often, someone decides to cross anyway — to trespass into the forbidden space not to conquer, but to listen.

This is the sacred art of going where love has been told not to go.

Father Desmond McAllister, an ageing Catholic priest in Belfast's Falls Road parish, knew the sound of grief as intimately as breath. During the height of The Troubles in the 1980s, his days were bookended by sacraments and sorrow.

He administered the Eucharist in the stillness of morning, and by afternoon delivered last rites for young men whose names he'd baptised years before. He christened infants into a world where their fathers sat behind the walls of Maze Prison. He knew every alleyway, every bullet hole, every bloodstain in his parish as well as he knew the words of the liturgy.

The air in Falls Road was thick with a tension you could taste — coal smoke, damp concrete, and fear. It was a world of impediments, both visible and unseen. And no wall was higher — or colder — than the one around Brendan Lynch.

Brendan was a known member of the IRA, a man whose reputation for violence was matched only by his silence. Locals had a name for him: Brendan the Wall. Nothing, they said, ever got through.

He had just lost his brother in a retaliatory attack by the loyalist Ulster Volunteer Force (UVF). Word on the street was that Brendan was planning revenge — an act that would surely ignite another round of bloodshed.

Upon hearing this, Father Desmond made a decision that was not only risky but unthinkable.

He decided to trespass. He sent a message through a parishioner, inviting Brendan Lynch to tea.

"Justice is what love looks like in public. Tenderness is what love feels like in private."— Cornel West.

To trespass is to cross a boundary where you are not authorised. It is, technically, a violation.

And yet, this is the very nature of God.

Throughout Scripture, God is a trespasser. He consistently crosses the boundaries we construct — cultural, ritual, geographic, even theological. He does this not to erase difference, but to restore dignity, relationship, and his own divine presence where it is least expected. His holiness is not separation for its own sake; it is a love with a gravitational pull, constantly trespassing across our self-imposed lines. We see this in the life of Jesus, who made holy trespass his ministry. When he touched a leper, he was not merely healing a man's skin; he was violating ritual purity laws to restore that man to his community, trespassing against a wall of religious exclusion. When he travelled into Samaria, he did not skirt enemy territory; he walked straight into it, trespassing over centuries of ethnic hostility to speak with a woman burdened by a scandalous past, treating her not as an outcast, but as a theologian. When the disciples bolted the door in fear after his crucifixion, the Holy Spirit did not honour their self-imposed boundary. The Spirit trespassed, breaking into their locked room not with condemnation, but with a breath of peace. God never honours our fear-built boundaries more than he honours the desperate needs of a human heart.

Father Desmond's invitation to Brendan the Wall was not an act of reckless idealism; it was an imitation of this divine, trespassing love. This kind of love is not a vague feeling. In my own journey from the chapel floor, I have come to see it as a way of being in the world — a set of spiritual orientations. I have come to recognise that this boundary-dissolving love is built upon seven core postures:

Hospitality Without Agenda: This is the quiet practice of opening your door — and your heart — with no bait and no hook. It is the choice to create a sanctuary where others can be long before they behave or believe. It is the extra chair at the table, the unguarded conversation, rooted in the biblical call to "show hospitality to strangers, for by doing so some have entertained angels without knowing it."

Sacrificial Listening: This is the choice to hear someone with no plan to reply, rebut, or rescue. It is the difficult, holy work of sitting in another's pain, especially when that pain accuses you, implicates your own tribe, or contradicts your worldview. It is the discipline of silencing your own agenda to truly receive theirs, of being "quick to listen, slow to speak, slow to become angry."

Leading with Lament: This is the posture of grieving before preaching. In a world that rushes to offer solutions and cheap optimism, leading with lament means choosing to mourn with those who mourn. It dignifies the wound rather than racing to cover it. It is the sacred pause that honours the pain — remembering that before Jesus resurrected Lazarus, he first stood before his tomb and wept.

Proximity Over Performance: This is the choice to value a quiet relationship over public optics. It is the willingness to step into messy, complicated spaces — privately, without fanfare, and not for credit — simply to be with another person in their reality. It may mean disappointing your own tribe for the sake of presence, just as Jesus was condemned by religious leaders for dining with tax collectors.

Naming Without Shaming: This is the art of telling the truth in a way that does not make the other person an enemy. It is the firm belief that one can name harm, history, and injustice without stripping the perpetrators of their own humanity. It is truth wrapped in dignity, a posture that disarms defensiveness and opens the door to repentance, echoing Jesus's words: "Neither do I condemn you. Go and sin no more."

Slow Advocacy: This is the willingness to lose speed in order to carry someone else's burden. In an age demanding instant results and viral moments, slow advocacy resists the urge to "go big." It chooses instead to walk with someone at their own pace, trusting that justice done with people is always more lasting than justice done to them.

Radical Curiosity: This is the choice to remain open to the story that challenges your own. It is not a descent into relativism where all truths are equal; it is an act of reverence, an admission that you do not possess the full picture. It flows from the belief that the opposite of love is not hate, but a hardened certainty that you have nothing left to learn from another. It is the posture of Jesus, who so often asked, "What do you want me to do for you?" — not because he did not know, but because he wanted to honour the desire of the person before him.

These postures are not theories; they are the practices Father Desmond embodied, armed with nothing but a kettle and a listening heart. Brendan Lynch arrived late, his wariness a palpable force field. He entered the simple rectory like a man entering a trap. The priest's table was set with the basics of Irish life: bread, marmalade, and mugs of strong, hot tea. The air in the small room was thick with a thousand unsaid things, with the ghosts of a generation of lost boys.

"The beginning of love is the will to let those we love be perfectly themselves." — Thomas Merton.

At first, there was only silence, punctuated by the clink of a spoon against ceramic. This was Father Desmond's first act of holy trespass: Sacrificial Listening. He did not fill the silence with platitudes or prayers. He let it be, absorbing Brendan's coiled anger and grief without trying to fix it. He simply poured the tea. This was Hospitality Without Agenda. There was no Bible on the table, no ulterior motive. Just a quiet, human invitation to share a moment of warmth in a cold, violent world.

Finally, Brendan spoke, his voice a low growl. "Tea? With you?" he scoffed, a cold, bitter sound. "You think a priest can fix this?"

"Not fix," Father Desmond replied softly. "Just listen."

And slowly, haltingly, they began to talk. Not about politics, not about the IRA or the UVF, but about their mothers, the shared grief of their city, and the insatiable war that swallowed their boys. The priest did not correct Brendan's narrative. He did not moralise about the cycle of violence. He simply listened, embodying the posture of Proximity Over Performance. He was not there as a religious authority to perform his role; he was there as one man sitting with another man's pain.

At one point, Brendan's hand trembled as he gripped his mug, the ceramic rattling against the saucer. "If I don't do something," he said, his voice tight with rage, "I'll explode."

This was the critical moment. The old way would have been to preach, to warn, to condemn. But Father Desmond, leading with Lament for the pain he heard in Brendan's voice, chose a different path. He looked the IRA member in the eye and said, "Then let's make sure what explodes is the silence between us, not more young men."

In that single sentence, Desmond practised Naming Without Shaming. He named the destructive path Brendan was on ("more young men") but did so in a way that invited him into a shared, constructive alternative ("the silence between us").

That conversation over tea did not end The Troubles. But it was a small act of demolition against the great wall of hate. Brendan Lynch never pulled the trigger to avenge his brother. Months later, he became a key figure in mediating a local neighbourhood ceasefire, his credibility with his own tribe allowing him to do what no outsider could.

He once ran into Father Desmond on the street. "I still don't believe everything you believe, Father," he said, a shadow of a smile on his face. "But that cup of tea might've saved my life."

From a conflict-resolution perspective, Desmond's intervention was a masterclass in de-escalation. In cycles of retaliatory violence, both sides are trapped in a self-perpetuating story of grievance and righteous anger. Top-down peace efforts often fail because they never reach the wounded core of human pain. Desmond's act of holy trespass created a third space — a neutral, human-scale environment where a different kind of conversation could take root. By offering dignity and listening without judgement, he depolarised the encounter and allowed Brendan to glimpse a future beyond the next act of revenge. He did not try to solve the whole conflict; he simply tried to save one man — and in doing so, may have saved many more.

The power in that room did not belong to the priest with his theology or the paramilitary with his gun. The power was in the vulnerability itself — in one man's willingness to sit, unarmed, across from danger with nothing but tea and a listening heart.

It was a reflection of the Incarnation itself. God did not shout solutions from heaven; he entered the mess of our world, sat at our tables, and listened to our pain. This is the source of all true peace-making. It does not begin with a treaty; it begins with the radical, terrifying, and holy act of sharing a cup of tea with your adversary.

But the art of holy trespass is not confined to priests or peacemakers in war zones. It is a posture available to every one of us — in the quiet conflicts that unfold inside our own homes.

Consider Angela, a single mother in Chicago. Her son, Jordan — once bright and affectionate — had dropped out of college and, over time, stopped talking to her. Their communication shrank to the occasional, clipped text. Years passed in silence.

When the pandemic struck, and Jordan lost his job, Angela's first instinct was to rush in with advice — with "I told you so" and a plan to fix everything. But she resisted.

Instead, she reached out with a simple act of trespass against the wall between them: "No expectations. Just want to know how you're doing. Want to come for lunch?"

To her surprise, he replied with one word: "Ok."

The first lunch was painfully awkward. But Angela practised Hospitality Without Agenda. She did not ask about jobs or responsibility. She simply cooked his favourite meal — biryani — and offered Sacrificial Listening.

By the third lunch, something had shifted. Jordan finally looked her in the eye and said quietly, "I thought you were only ever disappointed in me."

Angela fought back tears. This was the moment for Radical Curiosity. Instead of defending herself, she asked, "Maybe I was more scared than disappointed. But I'm not now. I just want to know who you're becoming."

That single, curious sentence cracked open what years of advice never could. They now meet once a week. Jordan has not figured everything out, but they are rebuilding — one small, holy trespass of grace at a time.

Family systems often hold the hardest walls of all — built from old wounds, unspoken rules, and assigned roles that have hardened over the years. Angela's story shows how one person can shift an entire system simply by changing their own posture. By moving from fixing (which

Jordan heard as judgement) to listening and curiosity, she replaced the energy of conflict with the energy of connection.

"To love someone is to learn the song in their heart and sing it back to them when they have forgotten." — Arne Garborg

To trespass, in the legal sense, is to step where you are not authorised. But holy trespass

means stepping where fear has declared a no-go zone — whether that zone is marked by race, ideology, grief, faith, or silence.

Boundary-dissolvers are not reckless; they are deliberate, gentle, and persistent. They create sanctuaries in kitchens, on pavements, in boardrooms, and in prison cells. Wherever walls have replaced welcome, they show up — not with force, but with presence. They knock on doors long locked, believing someone inside might be waiting for the sound. Because the walls that divide us — no matter how high or how old — are often just waiting for someone brave enough to knock.

Some boundaries are guarded by armies. Others with silence. But the first act of peace is always the same: a knock on the door, a seat at the table, a question asked without demand.

In the next chapter, we confront the power of that simple question.

FIELD GUIDE:
CHAPTER 6 INTEGRATION

The Practice of Holy Trespass

The art of holy trespass is learned not by study, but by practice.

It begins with small, deliberate choices to move towards connection instead of away from it.

Use these tools this week to begin your training as a Boundary-Dissolver.

1. Theological Meditation Point

Carry this definition of holy trespass with you.

Let it reframe your understanding of what it means to love courageously in a divided world.

"The walls that fear has declared a no-go zone are the very places where God calls me to practise holy trespass — not with force, but with the quiet, disarming presence of love that honours the person on the other side of the divide."

2. Questions for Reader Practice

Set aside time for a prayerful and honest reflection.

The goal is not to force yourself into a high-stakes confrontation, but to gently identify the next faithful step in your own life.

- Think of a significant wall in your own life — a strained relationship with a family member, a colleague you avoid, or a group you misunderstand.

Which of the seven postures feels like the most needed — and most difficult —first step towards knocking on that wall?

- Father Desmond practised Sacrificial Listening by absorbing Brendan's anger without trying to fix it.
- When was the last time you truly listened to someone you disagreed with, without planning your rebuttal while they were speaking?
- What happened in that conversation?
- Angela risked further rejection from her son, Jordan, by extending an invitation with "no expectations."

What is the primary risk — rejection, misunderstanding, discomfort — that holds you back from practising holy trespass more often?

3. Mini-Guide for Daily Embodying: The Practice of One Open Chair

Before you attempt a full Dinner Table Diplomacy, this small practice will help you build the core muscle of Hospitality Without Agenda.

Step 1: Identify an Opportunity: The goal is to create a small space of belonging for someone, with no strings attached.

This week, identify one simple opportunity to do so.

It could be inviting a new co-worker to join you for a coffee break, asking a neighbour you rarely speak with how their day is going, or sending that "no-expectations" text to a friend you've lost touch with — just as Angela did.

Step 2: Release the Agenda. As you make this small offering, consciously release any desired outcome. Your goal is not to get a specific response — not a thank-you, not a reciprocal invitation, not even a particularly deep conversation. Your entire practice is simply to hold a chair open for a moment, creating a tiny sanctuary in a walled-off world. Notice how it feels to give without an agenda.

AGAPE LAB #6: Dinner Table Diplomacy

The seven postures of a Boundary Dissolver are best learned not by theory, but by practice.

This lab is your first practical, low-stakes step into the art of holy trespass.

Dinner Table Diplomacy is the simple act of intentionally sharing a meal with someone from a different tribe — someone whose political view, religious belief, or life experience differs from your own.

The goal is not to debate, persuade, or even agree.

The goal is to practise Hospitality Without Agenda and Sacrificial Listening.

This exercise will guide you through each stage:

1. How to extend the invitation so it feels like a gesture of welcome, not a confrontation.
2. How to prepare the space — physically and emotionally — for curiosity, not conversion.
3. Conversation prompts that encourage storytelling over arguing.
4. Ways to close the evening with gratitude rather than resolution.
5. Your dinner table becomes a training ground for peace — a small, sacred rehearsal for the world we hope to build.

Chapter 7
The Currency of Curiosity

The night my world shattered on that chapel floor, God did not meet me with arguments, doctrines, or answers. My prayers were fists — rage and accusation pounding against the altar. And in response, I did not feel a lecture or a rebuttal. I felt only a quiet, patient presence.

In the silence that followed my shouting, it seemed as though God was not demanding repentance, but gently asking a deeper question — one that pulsed beneath all my pain:

What is the story of this wound?

I was beginning to learn that God's love often arrives not as a statement, but as a question. It doesn't seek to win a debate, but to know a soul. This divine curiosity — the kind that makes space for our truth to surface — is the most powerful tool for crossing the walls we build. It is the currency of a kingdom where being known is more important than being right.

You can win an argument and still lose a person. But ask the right question, and you might just gain their soul.

In a world of sharpened opinions and fortified ideologies, curiosity is the last form of rebellion — and perhaps the first act of repair.

We met at a faith and climate conference in Geneva — a place where good intentions and deep-seated resentments often shared the same recycled air. I was there to speak on a panel about community stewardship and the theology of creation care.

He was on a panel about responsible transition.

His name was Karl — a retired coal engineer from the United States — and in my mind, he was already the villain of my story.

Before he even spoke, I had cast him. He represented everything I believed was wrong with global climate inaction: denialism dressed up as pragmatism, economic justifications for ecological ruin, arrogance disguised as expertise.

And when he finally did speak, his words only confirmed my bias.

As he talked about how African nations "need infrastructure before regulation," I felt my jaw tighten and my heart harden. My mind wasn't listening — it was reloading.

That evening, at the conference dinner, we happened to be seated at the same table. The universe, it seems, has a wicked sense of humour.

I resolved to remain silent — a quiet protest.

He asked where I was from, and I told him. Then, my own anger — masquerading as courage — spilled out.

Leaning forward, my voice edged with accusation, I asked,

"Do you ever wonder how many communities like mine had to choke on smoke while you built that energy empire?"

A heavy silence settled over the table. Someone took an awkward, loud sip of wine.

I had drawn my line.

Then Karl looked at me, his expression unreadable.

"Can I ask you a question?" he said.

I braced myself for the counter-attack. But instead came this:

"What's the one story from your childhood that made you care so much about air?"

That question — simple, unexpected, disarming — was a perfect example of radical curiosity in action. It is the core tool of holy trespass.

Notice that Karl did not defend his position. He did not challenge my premise.

He did something far more powerful: he crossed the wall of ideology to honour the story behind it.

This is the very method of Jesus.

"The primary cause of suffering is not ignorance, but certainty." — Anthony de Mello.

Jesus — the Word made flesh, the One who embodied all truth — asked over three hundred questions in the Gospels. He did this not because He lacked knowledge, but because He understood that a statement can be rejected, but a genuine question requires a relationship.

When Jesus asked questions, He was not interrogating; He was liberating.

His curiosity was a form of love — a way of creating sacred space for a person's truth to rise to the surface.

When He asked, "Who do you say that I am?" He could have simply declared himself the Messiah.

Instead, He invited His friends into discovery. He entrusted the foundation of His Church not to the certainty of a declaration, but to the vulnerability of a relationship.

Likewise, when the legal experts tried to trap Him with, "Which is the greatest commandment?" Jesus didn't react defensively. He reframed their legalism around love itself — turning their test into a mirror of their hearts.

Jesus's questions were love in disguise. Whether He was asking, "Do you want to be made well?" or "Why are you afraid?" or "Whose image is on this coin?" — He was consistently dismantling hierarchy, restoring voice, and replacing judgement with presence.

His curiosity was His way of saying: You matter enough to be asked. And I am willing to stay for the answer.

"Compassion is not a relationship between the healer and the wounded. It's a relationship between equals." — Pema Chödrön

Consider the encounter with the rich young ruler in the Gospel of Mark.

Here was a man who had everything — wealth, status, religious perfection. He asked Jesus, "What must I do to inherit eternal life?" Jesus responded with a counter-question: "Why do you call me good? No one is good except God alone."

He unsettled the man's categories and invited him to think more deeply.

After the man listed the commandments he had kept, the Gospel adds a breathtaking line:

"Jesus looked at him and loved him."

From that place of love — not condemnation — came the invitation: "Go, sell everything you have and give to the poor. Then come, follow me."

The man went away sad. But the beauty of the story lies not in his failure; it lies in the method. Jesus did not coerce — He created space for freedom. He offered truth without control, love without manipulation.

That is divine curiosity: the courage to ask, and the humility to let someone walk away.

Back in that conference room in Geneva, I was the rich young ruler — wealthy in my own righteousness.

Karl's question — "What's the one story from your childhood that made you care so much about air?" — was the loving, disarming invitation that bypassed all my defences.

It didn't challenge my intellect; it called to my humanity.

So, I told him.

I told him about my grandmother's wheezing lungs, about the smog that rolled through our village during harmattan season, about waking up dizzy and believing that choking on air was normal.

He listened. Truly listened. No rebuttals. No excuses. Just silence — and empathy.

Then he shared his own story:

"When I was a boy, my dad worked in a coal mine. He came home coughing every night. Black dust under his fingernails and in the lines of his face. My mum cried each time he left for his shift. So, I became an engineer. I thought I could make it better. Safer. I thought I could fix it from the inside… But somewhere along the way, I think I lost the plot."

We talked until midnight.

By the end of the conference, we co-authored a joint statement on ethical infrastructure — a vision that included not only data and regulation, but memory and story.

We still disagree on many things, but we no longer do so from behind our walls.

The turning point was one question.

It wasn't, "Why do you believe what you believe?" — which invites argument.

It was, "What shaped you?" — which invites a soul.

What Karl did for me was an act of holy disarmament. My mind had been an armed fortress, ready to fire. But his question wasn't an assault; it was an invitation — to step out into the clearing of shared humanity, where stories rise like mist and no ideology casts a shadow.

He understood a truth that every peacemaker eventually learns: Facts rarely change a person's mind, but vulnerability can change a person's heart. His curiosity didn't target my intellect; it touched my story. And that is where transformation always begins.

This is the humility of holy curiosity — the grace to admit that the person in front of you is more complex than the label you've given them. It is the wisdom to believe their story holds a fragment of truth you do not yet possess.

"True wisdom is knowing you know nothing and remaining open to everyone." — Saint Isaac the Syrian.

This power is not reserved for conferences or councils. It is most needed — and most transformative — around our own kitchen tables.

Lena, a single mother and school vice-principal, was at war with her daughter, Grace.

At nineteen, Grace had dropped out of university and moved in with a partner Lena didn't approve of. What followed was a painful cycle of shouting, slamming doors, and, eventually, silence.

Lena tried everything: texts full of advice, long voicemails, even a Bible-verse-a-day campaign. Nothing worked. Finally, broken and exhausted, she confessed her failure to her therapist.

The therapist listened, then said gently:

"You're asking your daughter to return to your truth. Have you ever asked her what hers is?"

That night, Lena invited Grace for a walk. Halfway through the park, she took a deep breath and asked: "Grace, I've spent two years telling you who you're not — and I'm sorry. I want to know… who are you becoming?"

Grace froze — and then began to cry, not in anger, but in relief.

They sat on a bench for an hour while Grace talked about fear, shame, freedom, and failure.

Lena practised Sacrificial Listening. She didn't interrupt. She didn't theologise. She just listened.

A week later, Grace moved back home. Not because she had to — but because, for the first time in years, she felt safe enough to. What Lena's therapist gave her was a generative question.

In leadership and psychology, we distinguish between questions that close a conversation and those that open it.

- Judgemental questions — "Why did you do that?" or "Can't you see you're wrong?"— create defensiveness.
- Generative questions — "Who are you becoming?", "What can we learn from this?" "What matters to you about this?"— create possibility.

Generative questions shift focus from the past (blame) to the future (potential).

Lena's shift transformed a family system trapped in accusation into one capable of healing.

Judgement is fast. Curiosity is slow. Judgement reduces a person to a label. Curiosity restores their complexity. It whispers: Tell me more. What don't I understand yet? What would love sound like if I began with a question instead of a statement?

When Jesus walked the earth asking questions, He wasn't seeking information — He was creating sacred space. He was seeking souls. He was modelling a way of being that trusts that truth can rise in people who don't yet trust their own voice.

When we choose to do the same — whether across a boardroom table, a dinner table, or the space between generations — we participate in that same sacred act. We become holy ground.

The deepest truths aren't shouted. They're drawn out by a patient question.

In the next chapter, we explore what happens when that question is posed not across a table, but within the ache of our own body. What if the next wall we must trespass is the one between mind and flesh?

FIELD GUIDE:
CHAPTER 7 INTEGRATION

Practising Holy Curiosity

We have learned that the shortest distance between two people is a shared story — and the key that unlocks that story is curiosity. Use these tools this week to practise the art of asking questions that build bridges, not walls.

1. Theological Meditation Point

Carry this powerful contrast with you into your conversations this week. Let it be a gentle interruption whenever you feel the pull toward judgement.

Judgement is fast; it reduces a person to a label or a position. Curiosity is slow; it restores the complexity and dignity of a human soul. My goal in a difficult conversation is not to win the argument, but to create a sacred space for another's story to be heard.

2. Questions for Reader Practice

Set aside time for an honest look at your own conversational habits.

The goal is to notice where you may be building walls with statements when you could be opening doors with questions.

- In your most important relationships, what is your default posture when disagreement arises? Are you listening to understand, or listening for a chance to reply, rebut, and win?
- Think of a strained relationship in your life. Like Lena with her daughter Grace,
- have your attempts to connect been focused on telling them your truth?
- What might happen if you simply asked, with a sincere heart,
- "I want to know — who are you becoming?"
- Being curious requires releasing certainty and control. What are you afraid you might lose — or be forced to confront — if you were to become radically curious with someone you've labelled an enemy?

3. Mini-Guide for Daily Embodying: From "Why" to "What"

Before you attempt a full Story-Swap Walk, this small practice will help you build the core muscle of generative questioning in your everyday conversations.

Step 1: Identify an Opportunity

Think of one person in your life this week with whom conversations often feel tense, superficial, or predictable.

Step 2: Reframe the Question

The next time you speak, notice your instinct to ask a "Why" question that demands justification (e.g. "Why do you believe that?").

Intentionally replace it with a "What" or "How" question that invites a story.

Instead of Karl asking Zebedee, "Why are you so angry about coal?",

he asked, "What's the one story from your childhood that made you care so much about air?"

Try a similar shift: rather than "Why are you so worried about X?", ask "What's your earliest memory of feeling worried about X?" The practice is simple: change the question — then quietly notice what happens.

AGAPE LAB #7: The Story-Swap Walk

This lab puts the currency of curiosity directly into your hands. It is a structured practice for trading stories, not opinions, with someone whose views differ from your own.

The core exercise: invite someone from a different tribe on a walk. Walking side-by-side naturally diffuses the confrontational energy of a face-to-face debate.

The Rules Are Simple

1. For the first half of the walk, one person asks questions; the other tells the stories that have shaped their life and views.
2. Halfway through, you switch roles.
3. You are not permitted to argue, correct, or counter. Only to listen and ask follow-up questions beginning with what or how.
4. End by thanking each other for the courage to share, not for agreeing.

This lab provides a list of generative questions to guide your walk — questions that help you move beyond debate and into discovery. It is a practical step towards learning that the shortest distance between two people is, indeed, a shared story.

Chapter 8
The Counter-Physics of the Kingdom

Why Weakness Is Power and Trespass Is Strength

We live in a world that worships strength, rewards dominance, and fears vulnerability. But what if the most world-changing force was not might, but meekness?

What if history bends not under the weight of power, but under the quiet tremble of love that refuses to retaliate?

Birmingham, Alabama, spring 1963. A fortress of white supremacy. Segregation wasn't just culture — it was law. The city's Commissioner of Public Safety, Eugene "Bull" Connor, ruled with fire hoses, police dogs, and jail cells. His was the physics of worldly power: force plus fear equals control.

Into that fortress walked Dr Martin Luther King Jr., Reverend Fred Shuttlesworth, and the Southern Christian Leadership Conference — armed with a strategy that, by every worldly measure, looked suicidal. They confronted the machinery of racial violence not with bullets or bombs, but with the softest, most vulnerable weapon imaginable: the non-violent presence of their own bodies.

When adult protests stalled under the weight of threats and firings, a daring decision was made: the children would march. To critics, it was reckless — sending the young to face Connor's brutality. But Dr King saw it as an act of redemption, not desperation. He called it "redeeming the soul of the nation." He was placing his trust not in the physics of empire, but in the counter-physics of the Kingdom.

On the morning of 2 May 1963, hundreds of African-American children — some as young as seven — walked out of school. They gathered at the 16th Street Baptist Church, dressed not in armour, but in pressed shirts and Sunday dresses, their faces a blend of fear and resolve.

Their young voices rose in song, echoing through the sanctuary:

"Ain't gonna let nobody turn me 'round, turn me 'round, turn me 'round…"

Then, hand in hand, they marched out of the church — and into history.

I remember reading Paul's words to the church in Corinth: "My power is made perfect in weakness."

I didn't read it as comfort — I read it as contradiction.

The world had taught me that weakness was something to be conquered. Power meant capacity — economic, political, spiritual, emotional. But here was Paul, unveiling the scandalous mathematics of the Kingdom.

This is holy maths. It defies every law of self-preservation. Paul doesn't say that God's power replaces our weakness, or compensates for it. He says God's power is perfected through it. The weakness itself becomes the very site where divine strength is revealed.

"The logic of the Cross is not the logic of the market or the empire. It is the logic of seed falling into the ground and dying, so that something greater may live."— Dorothee Sölle

The Cross is the ultimate contradiction in the physics of power. At Golgotha, Rome displayed its might — law, violence, empire. And yet, Jesus — silent, stripped, surrendered — absorbed all that force without returning it in kind. In that act of non-retaliatory suffering, He disarmed violence and death forever.

The place of ultimate worldly failure — shame, loss, execution — became the very axis of human redemption.

This is the mystery at the heart of everything Jesus taught:

"Blessed are the meek," not the conquerors, "for they will inherit the earth."

"The first shall be last, and the last first." "Whoever loses their life for my sake will find it."

Each statement reverses the gravitational pull of human power.

Jesus was not romanticising weakness for its own sake; He was revealing a new kind of power — non-violent, soul-strong, justice-revealing power that subverts fear, pride, and domination not by overpowering them, but by refusing to play their game.

In the Kingdom's counter-physics, vulnerability does not strip power away — it reveals it. The softest thing can split stone. The gentlest posture can, in the right moment, reorder empires. And those the world calls "weak" have always been the ones to shift its moral axis.

Look again at the crucifixion. From the outside, it is a scene of utter defeat.

The disciples have fled. Peter, the rock, has fractured into denial. Judas has sold his loyalty for silver. The religious authorities have conspired with the empire. The crowd that shouted "Hosanna" now mocks.

Above Him hangs a sign, meant as a joke: "King of the Jews." Before Him, soldiers gamble for His last possession. He hangs between two criminals — a public spectacle of humiliation. Every ounce of worldly power is aligned against Him. By every measure, He is the weakest man in Jerusalem.

And what does He do with that moment of absolute powerlessness? He does not call down legions of angels. He does not curse His executioners.

He speaks.

"Father, forgive them, for they know not what they do."

Radical forgiveness — in the face of murder.

To the thief beside Him — a man with no time left to repent or prove his worth — He offers a promise:

"Today you will be with me in paradise."

Radical inclusion — in the face of death.

This is power made perfect in weakness. A power that absorbs hatred and returns love, absorbs violence and returns pardon, absorbs death itself — and returns life.

As the children marched out of the 16th Street Baptist Church, they were met with the full force of Bull Connor's worldly power. Police lined the streets. German shepherds barked, straining at their leashes. Then, on Connor's order, the firefighters opened the valves on their hoses. Water jets, powerful enough to strip bark from trees, slammed into the small bodies of the children. A nine-year-old boy named James Stewart Jr. was thrown to the ground by the blast, his body skidding across the pavement like a rag doll.

In the logic of the world, the story should have ended there. Force meets weakness; force wins. But then the counter-physics of the Kingdom took over.

The boy, clothes soaked and body bruised, stood up. His fists never clenched. He did not run.

He simply returned to the line with his fellow marchers.

That image — and hundreds like it — was captured by photographers and television crews. The televised scenes from Birmingham, broadcast into living rooms across America and around the world, pierced the conscience of a nation.

The United States could no longer sell its global image as a beacon of freedom while its citizens watched fire hoses turned on eleven-year-olds for the "crime" of wanting to eat at the same lunch counter as white people. Bull Connor's moral authority, with all his dogs and hoses, evaporated in an instant.

The weakness of the children became a mirror, forcing America to confront the ugliness of its own soul.

Public opinion shifted. A previously hesitant President John F. Kennedy declared segregation a "moral crisis" that he could no longer ignore. The campaign in Birmingham became the catalyst for the landmark Civil Rights Act of 1964.

The children — armed with nothing but songs, courage, and the dignity of their presence — accomplished what bombs, lawsuits, and politics could not. Their meekness had moved a mountain. Their weakness had become a world-changing power.

The Birmingham Campaign was a masterclass in what some strategists call "moral jujitsu."

In jujitsu, one does not meet force with equal force; one uses the opponent's momentum against them.

Dr King and his colleagues knew that Bull Connor's only language was brute force. By refusing to retaliate, they denied him the moral cover he needed. They created a public theatre in which the only visible violence belonged to the state. The very hoses meant to crush the movement became the engines that propelled its message across the world. Their vulnerability became their greatest strategic asset.

I have come to see this as the spiritual genius of "turning the other cheek." It is not passivity or cowardice. It is a courageous, dignified refusal to mirror the dehumanisation of one's oppressor.

By not retaliating, the children of Birmingham preserved their moral and spiritual integrity. They declared,

"You can assault our bodies, but you cannot have our souls. We will not become like you."

Their march was not merely a political protest; it was a worship service in the streets — a living act of resurrection in the shadow of empire.

"Non-violence is a powerful and just weapon which cuts without wounding and ennobles the man who wields it." — Martin Luther King Jr.

This counter-intuitive truth — that vulnerability can be a source of strength — is not confined to history's epic struggles. It can reset the culture of a family, a team, or even a corporation.

Keisha Liu was thirty-four when her celebrated AI start-up — a company she had built from the ground up — hit a wall. A major software release had failed. Key clients were threatening to leave. Investors were spooked. Her engineers were exhausted and afraid.

At the tense quarterly all-hands meeting, every instinct told Keisha to posture strength. The playbook was clear: project confidence, announce a pivot, reassure the team.

But as she stood before the whiteboard, she realised that would be a lie.

Taking a deep breath, she looked at her anxious employees and chose a different kind of power.

"Before we talk about solutions," she said quietly, "I need to say this — I'm afraid. I pushed us too fast. I didn't listen when some of you warned me. If we're going to survive this, I need your help, not your fear."

"Vulnerability is the birthplace of innovation, creativity, and change."
— Brené Brown.

A heavy silence followed. Then, something shifted. A senior developer — known for his cynicism — raised his hand.

"Thank you for saying that," he said. "Honestly, we've been holding back ideas because we thought failure wasn't allowed here."

That moment didn't fix the technical crisis, but it cracked the room open. Blame gave way to collaboration.

Within six months, the team — now operating with renewed trust — restructured their workflow, launched a successful open-source project, and secured new funding.

Investors cited not just the technology, but the honesty and health of the team's culture.

Keisha now speaks at tech conferences not about scaling fast, but about the power of slow trust — and the strategic advantage of a leader's vulnerability.

Her story reflects a paradigm shift in modern leadership. For decades, leadership meant control — the myth of the infallible commander. But research, popularised by thinkers like Brené Brown, shows that vulnerability is not weakness; it is the prerequisite for trust. And trust is the engine of innovation, collaboration, and resilience.

Keisha's confession was not a collapse of authority; it was the truest form of it.

The Kingdom's counter-physics, it turns out, is also sound business strategy.

The Kingdom's power is not in being the loudest voice in the room; it is in being the one who can absorb fear and give back grace. When we choose forgiveness over retaliation, confession over control, and trembling openness over clenched certainty — we shift the gravitational field of the moment itself.

The world says: dominate to win. The Gospel whispers: kneel to rise.

The Cross — once a Roman instrument of terror — now stands as history's most recognised symbol of hope. This is not soft power; this is resurrection power.

In a world obsessed with winning, the Kingdom invites a stranger victory — one born not from conquest, but from confession.

What if the next revolution doesn't begin with a protest, but with a question — asked by someone brave enough to lay their armour down?

In the next chapter, we meet the unlikely allies who dared to do exactly that.

FIELD GUIDE: CHAPTER 8 INTEGRATION

The counter-physics of the Kingdom is not a theory to be understood, but a reality to be embodied. This is resurrection power, and it can only be known through practice. Use these tools to shift your posture from one of worldly force to one of Kingdom strength.

1. Theological Meditation Point

Carry this re-framing of power with you this week. Let it be your compass in moments of conflict and fear.

The power of the world works by force, seeking to control and dominate. The power of God's Kingdom works through weakness, absorbing fear and returning grace. My true strength is revealed not in my capacity, but in my vulnerability.

2. Questions for Reader Practice

Set aside time to honestly examine your relationship with power. The goal is to see where you rely on the world's physics and where you might be invited to experiment with God's.

- What does the word power mean to you in your daily life? In what situations do you feel most powerful? In what situations do you feel most powerless?

- Keisha Liu chose vulnerability when her instinct was to posture strength. Think of a current challenge you are facing at work or at home. What would the worldly physics approach (asserting control, demanding to be right) look like? What might a counter-physics approach of vulnerability or confession look like in that same situation?
- The children in Birmingham risked their physical safety by choosing non-violence. What does choosing weakness (vulnerability, confession, apology) feel like it would cost you in your most difficult relationship or situation? What hidden strength might lie on the other side of that cost?

3. Mini-Guide for Daily Embodying: The Posture Swap

Before you undertake a full "Power Audit," this small practice will help you build the muscle of choosing a different kind of strength in low-stakes moments.

Step 1: Identify a Moment. Think of one common, low-stakes situation this week where your default is to assert power. This could be the need to win a minor argument with a spouse, the urge to prove you're right in a meeting, or the impulse to give unsolicited advice to a friend.

Step 2: Choose the "Weaker" Posture. In that moment, intentionally choose the posture that feels "weaker." Instead of delivering the winning point in the argument, try saying, "You've given me a lot to think about." Instead of insisting on your idea, try Keisha Liu's phrase: "Honestly, I might need some help with this." Instead of giving advice, simply listen. Notice the internal resistance you feel. Notice what happens in the conversation. The goal is not to become a doormat, but to experiment with the surprising strength found in letting go of control.

AGAPE LAB #8: The Power Audit:

We have all been trained to use worldly forms of power to get what we want—control, authority, intellect, anger, volume, or withdrawal. This lab is a personal inventory, a private "power audit" to help you see the tools you most often reach for. It will guide you through a reflection on a recent conflict or difficult situation in your own life. Identify the forms of worldly power you used, and then prayerfully consider one small area where you could experiment with the counter-physics of the Kingdom. Where could you choose to confess instead of control? Where could you show up with curiosity instead of certainty?

This is not a call to become a doormat, but a strategic invitation to discover the surprising strength that is made perfect in your weakness.

Chapter 9
The Terrible Freedom of Forgiveness

Some betrayals feel like death. But forgiveness — true, defiant forgiveness — is a resurrection. It doesn't erase the scar; it rewrites the ending.

Before I could ever forgive another, I first had to face the person I could not forgive — myself. For months after Jean's death, I lived inside a private cell of self-loathing.

The world could have offered me a thousand pardons, and I would have rejected every one of them, because the debt I carried felt absolute. The rage I felt was not outward; it was inward — a slow, corrosive fire that hollowed everything it touched.

It was only when I began to grasp the magnitude of the grace offered to me — a grace I did nothing to deserve — that I could even begin to release myself. The terrible freedom described in this chapter is not a theory for me; it is the ground upon which I learned to stand again.

Tasha, a mid-career architect in Toronto, described her own moment of discovery as a freezing over. It was late on a Tuesday night in her small but thriving firm, the office hushed except for the hum of her computer. For over a decade, she and her closest friend from grad school, Julian, had built something rare — a business rooted in ethics, creativity, and what she believed was unbreakable trust.

But a nagging discrepancy in the quarterly accounts led her down a rabbit hole of invoices and vendor logs. And there it was, illuminated by the cold blue light of her screen: a shell vendor account, a string of transactions, a six-year-long deception.

Julian had been embezzling from their firm — over $230,000, siphoned away in small, deliberate increments. The numbers were unambiguous.

When she confronted him the next day, he confessed under the weight of the evidence.

He offered a vague, hollow apology — and then vanished. No repayment, no explanation, no closure. Just silence.

He left Tasha alone in the wreckage of their shared dream. The betrayal was absolute.

In the weeks that followed, that freezing over became her new reality. A wall of ice encased her heart. Laughter felt performative. Trust — in her clients, her employees, even in her own judgement — evaporated.

She spent sleepless nights rereading old emails, torturing herself to pinpoint the exact moment the lies began. She fantasised about suing him, about shaming him publicly, about destroying his reputation as he had destroyed their company. The world — and all her well-meaning friends — told her she had every right.

"Don't you dare let it go," they said. "He doesn't deserve your forgiveness."

And they were right. He didn't.

But that was never the point.

"I thought hating him gave me control," Tasha told me later. "But it was just eating me alive."

This is the terrible lie of unforgiveness: it masquerades as power. It feels like control. We believe that by holding on to our rage — by replaying the injustice in our minds — we are keeping the person who hurt us locked inside a prison of our making.

But the bars of that prison are wrapped around our own souls.

"To forgive is to set a prisoner free and discover that the prisoner was you." — Lewis B. Smedes

The world often confuses forgiveness with forgetting — as if a wound so deep could simply be erased like chalk from a board. Or worse, it treats forgiveness as weakness, a passive way for "nice" people to move on without demanding justice.

But Christian forgiveness is not weak amnesia; it is rugged spiritual defiance.

In the tradition of Jesus, forgiveness is not a feeling. It is a decision — the raw, often agonising choice to cancel a debt that someone truly owes you.

A betrayal happened. A wound was inflicted. A debt was created. Justice demands repayment.

But forgiveness looks at the ledger and says: I will not make you pay. I will absorb the cost myself.

It does not say, "What you did is okay." It says, "What you did was profoundly wrong — but I refuse to let your wrongness define my future."

Jesus illustrated this spiritual physics in the Parable of the Unforgiving Servant.

It is a story of grotesque, almost comic contrast — meant to jolt us awake.

A servant is brought before his king, owing ten thousand talents — an astronomical, unpayable sum, worth millions today. Facing ruin, the servant falls to his knees and begs for mercy. The king, moved with compassion, does the unthinkable: he cancels the entire debt. The servant walks out a free man — the beneficiary of an absurd, undeserved grace.

Moments later, that same servant finds a fellow servant who owes him a few hundred silver coins — a pittance in comparison. He seizes him by the throat, demanding repayment. Despite the fellow servant's pleas for mercy — the very same pleas he himself had made to the king — he has the man thrown into prison until the small debt can be paid.

The parable is a violent, uncomfortable mirror. Jesus makes it clear: you cannot be a vessel of grace received and a fortress against grace extended. It's not merely a moral principle; it's a law of spiritual physics. The forgiven heart that cannot bring itself to forgive others reveals that it never truly grasped the magnitude of its own pardon.

And then, of course, there is the ultimate model — Jesus Himself. Bleeding, humiliated, nailed to a cross. His lungs filling with fluid, His body a canvas of imperial torture.

From that very instrument of shame and agony, He looks out at His mockers, accusers, and executioners, and speaks:

"Father, forgive them," He says, "for they know not what they do."

He does this not after they apologise, not after they change, but in the very midst of their violence.

Forgiveness here is not an emotional resolution reached after the pain has subsided; it is an act of cosmic resistance performed in the heart of pain itself.

Jesus models a divine, debt-cancelling love that declares with its final breath:

You will not make me become like you. I will not let your violence write the final word of my story.

This is the terrible freedom. And the path to resurrection, for all of us, runs straight through it.

Tasha's prayers were hollow. Her therapy sessions felt like picking at a wound that refused to close. The advice of her friends — to stay angry, to "never let it go" — only deepened her sense of imprisonment.

One sleepless night, after waking from yet another vivid dream of revenge, she opened her Bible and let it fall open where it may. Her eyes landed on Matthew 18 — the Parable of the Unforgiving Servant.

The king's question to the wicked servant seemed to leap off the page and pierce her heart:

"Should you not have had mercy on your fellow servant, just as I had mercy on you?"

She wept. Not because she suddenly felt mercy for Julian, but because, for the first time, she saw her own chains.

Her unforgiveness was the smaller debt — the hundred silver coins she was choking her own soul over — even as she herself had been forgiven the ten thousand talents of her own failings.

She did not forgive him that night. The process was non-linear, halting, and deeply costly.

But she began the work.

She started by simply saying the words aloud in the quiet of her apartment, once a day, even when she didn't feel them:

"I release you, Julian. I will not make you pay me back in my mind today."

She wrote him a long, detailed letter she never intended to send. In it, she listed every theft — not just the stolen money, but the stolen friendship, the stolen trust, the stolen years. She poured her grief and fury onto the page. And at the end, her hand trembling, she wrote words that were both a prayer and a decision: "You owe me more than you can ever repay. But today, I choose to cancel your debt."

Some days, she relapsed into bitterness. She would hear his name or see a project they had once worked on, and the familiar bile of rage would rise in her throat. In those moments, she repeated her mantra, clinging to it like a life raft:

"I release you. Not because you deserve it, but because I deserve to be free."

She never received restitution for the money he stole. But over many months, she received something far stranger — and infinitely more valuable: peace.

Six months later, she ran into Julian at a design expo. He looked older, his shoulders stooped, his eyes hollow. She saw him before he saw her.

Her heart didn't pound with rage; her mind didn't race with all the things she might say. There was only a quiet, weightless space inside her.

She didn't speak to him. She simply turned and walked away. "It didn't feel triumphant," she said. "It didn't feel like I'd won. It felt quiet — like laying down a heavy sword I'd been carrying for far too long."

Tasha's story reveals a profound psychological truth about unforgiveness. The rage we cling to feels like a weapon aimed at the person who hurt us, but in reality, it is self-poisoning. Chronic anger — the endless replay of betrayal — keeps our nervous system trapped in high alert. Her description of hatred eating her alive is not just metaphor; it is physiological fact.

Her decision to forgive, therefore, was not merely spiritual — it was strategic. It was the deliberate act of reclaiming her life from the story of her betrayal. She chose to prioritise her own freedom over her perpetrator's guilt. It was, in every sense, a resurrection.

The power of Tasha's forgiveness lay in its unilateral nature. It was not dependent on Julian's apology, remorse, or restitution. Had she waited for any of those, she might have waited forever, remaining a prisoner of his inaction. Instead, her forgiveness was a sovereign act — a quiet declaration of her own spiritual agency. She was imitating the grace of God, which flows toward us not because we are worthy, but because God is good.

The peace she experienced was not the triumphant calm of a battle won, but the deep, resonant peace the Bible calls shalom — a state of wholeness that arises not when our external circumstances are perfect, but when our inner world is rightly ordered with God.

"Forgiveness is not an occasional act; it is a constant attitude." — Martin Luther King Jr.

If forgiveness on a personal level is a war against the bitterness of our own souls,

what does it look like on a national scale, in the aftermath of catastrophe?

In the wake of the 1994 Rwandan Genocide — when nearly one million Tutsi were slaughtered by their Hutu neighbours in just 100 days — the question was not merely how to rebuild an economy, but how to rebuild a society. How do you sit in church next to the man who murdered your family?

In Nyamata, a town that witnessed some of the genocide's worst atrocities, survivors and perpetrators were forced to live side by side after the killing stopped. The government launched the Gacaca courts — a community-led justice system designed to encourage confession and restorative sentencing. But legal justice alone could not heal the wounds of the soul.

A deeper healing began in reconciliation workshops, often led by Christian trauma counsellors.

Survivors like Marie-Claire, whose husband and all of her children had been killed by their neighbour — a man named Pascal — began the slow, agonising work of processing their grief. After two years, Marie-Claire did something unthinkable: she asked to meet with Pascal.

They sat together beneath an acacia tree. He trembled as he confessed, in full detail, the story of his crimes. She listened. She wept. And then she spoke the words that would change both of their lives:

"I can never get my children back. But if I hold this hatred, I will never get my life back either.

I forgive you. I want to live again."

Pascal fell to his knees and sobbed.

Today, Marie-Claire and Pascal both tend the same community garden at their local church. Their story is now part of Rwanda's national healing curriculum. Forgiveness did not erase the past — it simply refused to let the past own the future.

As Marie-Claire has said:

"Forgiveness is not peace at first. It is a war against the bitterness in your own soul.

But when it wins, you are no longer a prisoner of the grave."

The Rwandan experience is a powerful testament to the necessity of restorative, rather than purely retributive, justice. Retributive justice asks, "What punishment does the offender deserve?" Restorative justice asks, "What must be done to heal the harm and repair the community?"

While holding perpetrators accountable is essential, punishment alone cannot rebuild the social fabric. Practices like the Gacaca courts and reconciliation workshops — which prioritise confession, truth-telling, and, where possible, forgiveness — are not "soft" on justice. They represent a more ambitious and enduring form of justice: one aimed at healing an entire society, not merely punishing individuals.

Forgiveness is not agreement. It is not denial. It is not instant. It is the blood-and-sweat work of holy trespass against the walls of our own wounds. It is the gritty, unglamorous, day-by-day decision to rewrite the ledger we carry in our souls.

"The weak can never forgive. Forgiveness is the attribute of the strong." — Mahatma Gandhi.

But it is the only power strong enough to end generational cycles of violence,

to shatter the walls of betrayal, and to birth something new and beautiful in the ashes of our deepest pain.

When we forgive, we do not pretend the pain didn't matter. We proclaim, with every fibre of our being, that God's grace matters more.

Forgiveness does not change the past. It dares to change the future.

In the next chapter, we confront the stories we carry — and how they carry us — until we dare to rewrite them.

FIELD GUIDE:
CHAPTER 9 INTEGRATION

Forgiveness is not a single event, but a difficult, courageous journey. It is a war waged against the bitterness in our own souls for the sake of our own freedom. Use these tools this week to take the first small, defiant steps on that path.

1. Theological Meditation Point

Carry this definition with you, especially in moments when you feel the pull of resentment. Let it reframe your understanding of what you are truly choosing.

Forgiveness is not a feeling I wait for; it is a decision I make. It is not saying, "What you did is okay." It is saying, "I refuse to let what you did continue to control my heart."

2. Questions for Reader Practice

Set aside time for this reflection. Be gentle with yourself. This is perhaps the most difficult work a human heart can do. The goal is simply to bring awareness to the debts you are carrying.

- Tasha had to name the specific debts Julian owed her before she could begin to cancel them. Who in your life holds a significant debt against you? Without judgement, simply name the person and the specific wound you are carrying.

- Tasha realised her hatred was a heavy sword she'd carried too long. What is the weight or cost of the unforgiveness you are carrying? How does it affect your body, your thoughts, or your other relationships?
- The Parable of the Unforgiving Servant hinges on the idea that we can only give what we have received. Reflect on a time you have been shown grace or forgiveness

when you didn't deserve it. How does that memory impact your willingness — or unwillingness — to extend forgiveness to others?

3. Mini-Guide for Daily Embodying: The Prayer of Release

Before attempting the deep work of The Forgiveness Ledger, this small, private practice can help you begin the internal process of letting go, using the very words that helped Tasha find her freedom.

Step 1: Acknowledge the Debt. Bring to mind the person and the wound you identified in the reflection questions. Take a moment to acknowledge the reality of the pain and anger you feel. Do not try to suppress it or pretend it isn't there.

Step 2: Practise Release. Once a day for the next three days, find a quiet moment. Sit down and open your hands, placing them palms-up on your lap as a physical posture of letting go. Take one deep breath and say Tasha's simple, powerful prayer aloud:

"I release you. Not because you deserve it, but because I deserve to be free."

You may not feel any different at first. The practice is not about achieving a feeling; it's about making a small, repeated choice for your own liberation.

AGAPE LAB #9: The Forgiveness Ledger

This lab is a private, guided journaling exercise designed to help you begin the rugged work of forgiveness. It is not a tool to force a feeling, but a practice to clarify a decision. You will be guided to create a ledger in your journal. On one side, honestly name the debts you are owed — write down the specific wounds and betrayals you are carrying. This act of naming is a vital first step.

On the other side, prayerfully consider the choice that Tasha made: the choice to cancel the debt. This lab will provide you with prompts, prayers, and meditations to help you sit with this difficult decision — not for the sake of the person who hurt you, but for the sake of your own terrible freedom.

Chapter 10
When Hospitality Hurts

What do you do when the bridge you built with your bare hands collapses beneath your feet?

When your deepest acts of love are met with suspicion — or silence?

For those who walk the path of reconciliation, rejection is not a possibility; it is a rite of passage.

I know this rite of passage intimately. In the weeks after my failure, as I knelt in the mud beside Jean's grieving mother, her silent sorrow felt like a judgment. The hope that had once lived in the eyes of Jean's brother had been replaced by quiet accusation.

My attempts to offer comfort were, at first, met with a coldness that felt like a slammed door. I had built a bridge of authority and confidence as a priest, and it had collapsed under the weight of my own fear.

Learning to show up with nothing but my brokenness — to simply be present in the ruins without trying to mend them — was the most painful and necessary lesson of my life.

For twelve years, Amina Youssef's life was a testament to the slow, stubborn work of hope. A Lebanese Christian peace activist, she had chosen to make her home in Tripoli — a city split by deep, jagged sectarian lines carved into its post–civil war soul: Sunni versus Alawite, Christian versus Muslim, neighbour versus neighbour.

In her early thirties, Amina began hosting dialogue circles in secret — small, sacred spaces where the city's warring identities could, if only for a few hours, be laid down.

She brought together imams and priests, former militia fighters hardened by violence and mothers softened by grief. In a room filled with the scent of coffee and cardamom, she offered food, Scripture, and poetry — believing that shared humanity was the only force strong enough to mend a broken city.

Over more than a decade, she built a fragile network of trust — tiny acts of healing layered like threadbare cloth over generational scars. She helped young fighters trade their guns for vocational training. She organised gestures of peace, such as planting olive trees along the former battle lines that once divided neighbourhoods. She once spent three sleepless days mediating a standoff over a disputed mosque, her calm presence a balm against the city's raw anger.

She was building a bridge — one person, one conversation, one olive tree at a time.

But in 2014, after a particularly brutal outbreak of violence in the Jabal Mohsen neighbourhood, Amina spoke at a televised public forum. She stood before the cameras, her heart heavy with her city's pain, and said the words she believed were the only path to true peace: "Both communities have blood on their hands. Reconciliation will only happen when we acknowledge this."

Those words, spoken from a heart dedicated to healing, lit a match to the very bridge she had spent her life building.

I have wept in the silence after trying to reconcile two people I loved, only to find myself blocked by both. I have stood at pulpits where my most heartfelt call for justice was met with stony silence and averted eyes. I have prayed for healing in rooms where, by all outward appearances, nothing changed at all.

And so, I say this with the certainty of a pastor who has the scars to prove it:

to follow the way of Jesus is to know the sharp, bitter sting of rejection.

The Gospel of John puts it plainly: "He came to that which was his own, but his own did not receive him."

This was not a passing detail in Jesus's story — it was its recurring refrain.

He was misunderstood and questioned by His own family.

He was laughed out of His hometown synagogue in Nazareth.

He was hunted by the very religious leaders who should have been His allies.

He was abandoned by His closest friends in His hour of greatest need.

And He was ultimately condemned and crucified by the same crowds He had healed and fed.

"To be rejected by your own is to know the Christ who wept over Jerusalem.

This, too, is sacred." — Henri Nouwen

Yet the most haunting moment of rejection in all of Scripture does not come from humanity's hands, but from the silence of God.

From the cross, in His final agony, Jesus cries out the ancient words of the Psalmist:

"My God, my God, why have you forsaken me?"

This cry is not a lapse of faith or a moment of doubt — it is the most radical act of spiritual honesty in history. It validates every human being who has ever felt abandoned in their suffering.

It is divine permission to say the unsayable — when the dinner table explodes into shouting, when the reconciliation dies mid-sentence, when the protest ends in silence and hatred seems to win.

The cry from the cross assures us: God is not afraid of our anguish, nor offended by our questions.

A theology of failure does not mean we stop building bridges. It means we learn that God lives in the rubble too.

The resurrection did not come to the disciples in a blaze of triumph. It came to them while they hid behind locked doors, paralysed by fear and failure. The risen Christ walked through their bolted rooms, bringing peace not to the victorious — but to the heartbroken.

The backlash against Amina was immediate and absolute. Both factions — united for the first time in their shared fury — turned on her. An imam who had once shared coffee with her publicly declared her "a traitor to the martyrs."

A Christian militia leader she had worked with called her "naïve and dangerous."

The death threats began to arrive: first as whispers, then as shouted words on the street, then as messages slipped under her door. Her home was vandalised. Her name was slandered in the press. The international donors who had funded her peace centre, spooked by the controversy, quietly withdrew their support. Finally, the municipal authorities, citing "security reasons", officially shut the centre down.

The bridge not only collapsed, but it was also burned.

The betrayal felt biblical in its scope. "I felt crucified by the very people I'd washed feet for," she said later. The years of stress and the trauma of rejection caused a complete collapse — spiritual and physical. She was diagnosed with severe adrenal burnout and, on her doctor's orders, withdrew from public life entirely. For two years, she lived in silence, her heart a landscape of ash and ruin.

Her recovery — her quiet resurrection — came not through a new strategic plan, but through Scripture. She attended a silent retreat at a mountain monastery, spending days meditating on a single story from Luke's Gospel: the disciples in a boat, caught in a furious storm, crying to a sleeping Jesus, "Master, master, we are perishing!"

When Jesus calmed the storm, He asked them, "Where is your faith?"

In that story, Amina found a new definition of faithfulness. It wasn't her job to control the storm or to guarantee safe arrival on the other side. Her job was simply to stay in the boat with Jesus — even when it felt like they were both going down.

She began again — but differently. Quietly. No grants. No press conferences. She started by meeting with just two mothers: one Sunni, one Alawite, both of whom had lost sons in the fighting. They met for coffee every week. They didn't talk about politics; they talked about their boys. They shared photos. They wept.

"I no longer seek to change a city," Amina, now in her fifties and working as a spiritual director, has said. "I seek to hold sacred space for two souls at a time. Jesus lost the crowds, but He still knelt to wash the feet of the few. So will I."

She had learned the hardest and most profound lesson of holy trespass: the bridge collapsed, but, as she says, "Christ builds resurrection paths where bridges fail."

"Faithfulness is not success. It is presence, even when the crowd disappears." — Eugene Peterson

Amina's story illustrates a painful dynamic often seen in protracted conflicts. The peacemaker, by insisting on shared humanity and shared responsibility, becomes a threat to the simple, unifying narratives of both sides.

For leaders of each faction, it is easier to maintain power by pointing to the absolute evil of the other and the absolute innocence of us. Amina, by saying "both communities have blood on their hands," violated this rule. She became a lightning rod — a single target for the unprocessed anger and grief of two entire communities. Her vilification was, in a tragic way, the first thing the two sides had agreed upon in years.

The profound shift in Amina's understanding of her mission was the key to her resilience. Her move from seeking to change a city to seeking to hold sacred space for two souls marks a movement away from a theology of worldly success and toward a theology of faithful presence.

Many of us burn out in ministry or activism because we tie our sense of faithfulness to measurable results. Amina learned to anchor hers in the act of showing up itself. This is the essence of mature faith: the ability to plant a seed without demanding to see the flower. It is the trust that resurrection happens on God's time — often in the quiet, unseen places — long after we have pronounced our own efforts a failure.

While few of us will face the danger Amina did, many of us will face the sting of rejection in our own attempts at bridge-building.

David, a middle-aged progressive pastor in Milwaukee, felt compelled to practise the principles of holy trespass. He decided to host a "Courageous Conversations" dinner at his home. The idea was simple but audacious: invite four members from his own progressive church and four from a neighbouring conservative evangelical church to share a meal and talk honestly about the issues dividing them — politics, race, theology.

He spent hours curating the guest list, hoping to find open-minded participants. He and his wife cooked a vast Ethiopian feast. He even printed quotes from both Martin Luther King Jr. and C. S. Lewis, placing them on the table as prompts for dialogue.

For forty-five minutes, it worked beautifully. They found common ground — talking about their children, their favourite Green Bay Packers moments, and the Psalms they turned to in times of trouble.

Then someone brought up immigration.

An elder from David's church spoke passionately about welcoming the stranger.

A man from the other church replied, his voice tight: "We have to protect our borders — our Christian faith in this nation depends on it." A seminary student from David's congregation shot back, "That sounds like xenophobia baptised in nationalism."

The air went cold. What followed was not dialogue but a descent into accusation. There was shouting. There was sarcasm. A chair toppled as one guest stormed out.

David was left alone in his dining room, staring at platters of untouched food and half-empty glasses. He sat there until one in the morning, replaying every moment, drowning in humiliation.

"I had opened my home as a sanctuary," he said later, "and it became a courtroom."

He vowed never to try again.

Three days later, a text appeared on his phone from one of the women from the conservative church:

"I have to be honest. I hated that night. I felt attacked and angry. But I haven't stopped thinking about it all week. Thank you for trying."

That single message was a lifeline.

"Hospitality isn't about creating harmony," David realised. "It's about creating an opportunity for courage. You can't control what people do with the invitation. But you can keep the table open."

"Hospitality is not about having the perfect table but making room for imperfect stories." — Parker J. Palmer

David's experience highlights a common pitfall in dialogue work. We often enter with hidden agendas, even noble ones — we want everyone to get along. We want harmony. But, as David learned, the goal of holy trespass isn't harmony; it's honesty.

The dinner was not a failure. It was a painful success. It revealed the true depth of division.

The single text message proved that the trespass was effective — it created a crack in someone's certainty, a space where light could enter. That is victory, even when it feels like defeat.

The measure of our faithfulness is not the response we receive; it is the offering we make.

Jesus did not rise from the dead because people finally believed in Him. He rose while His followers still hid in doubt and fear. His resurrection was not a reward for their success; it was a response to their failure.

So, when the dinner party ends in silence or shouting, when the peace initiative gets you slandered, when your outstretched hand is slapped away, when all your carefully constructed bridges fall — know this: Christ is there with you in the ruins. He is there in the rubble, planting seeds of resurrection you may never live to see bloom.

And He whispers to your exhausted, heartbroken soul:

"Well done, good and faithful servant. You did your part. You built the bridge. Leave the crossing to Me."

We long to see fruit. But sometimes all we are given is a seed.

In the next chapter, we explore how to live and lead when the harvest is invisible — and the applause never comes.

Field Guide:
Chapter 10 Integration

To follow Jesus is to know rejection. The path of a Boundary Dissolver is not a path of guaranteed success, but one of stubborn faithfulness. Use these tools to find God in the rubble and to cultivate a hope stronger than your circumstances.

1. Theological Meditation Point

Carry this redefinition of faithfulness with you, especially when you feel discouraged. Let it be the anchor for your hope.

My faithfulness is measured by the courage of my offering, not the harmony of the outcome.

God does not call me to control the storm; He calls me to stay in the boat with Him, even when the road gives way beneath my feet.

2. Questions for Reader Practice

Set aside time to reflect with compassion on your own experiences of failure and rejection. The goal is not to re-live the pain, but to find God's presence within it.

- Reflect on a time you tried to build a bridge — in a relationship, at work, or in your community — and it collapsed. Like David sitting at his ruined dinner table, what story did you tell yourself about that failure?

- Amina had to redefine her mission from changing a city to holding sacred space for two souls. How might you need to redefine success in a difficult relationship or situation, shifting your focus from the external outcome to your own faithful presence?
- Jesus's ministry was filled with rejection from His own people. How does the fear of failure or rejection keep you from taking risks of love and hospitality in your own life?

3. Mini-Guide for Daily Embodying: The Open Hand Offering

Before attempting the deeper work of The Resilience Ritual, this small practice helps you build the muscle of detaching your faithfulness from the results.

Step 1: Identify a Small Offering. Think of one simple, low-stakes act of hospitality or connection you can offer this week. It might be sending an encouraging text, giving a sincere compliment to a colleague, or sharing a vulnerable idea in a meeting.

Step 2: Practise the Release. Just before you act, hold your hands out in front of you, palms open, as a physical posture of offering. Whisper a short prayer: "God, I offer this freely. The outcome belongs to You." Then send the text, give the compliment, or share the idea — and consciously release your attachment to how it is received. The practice is not about achieving a response; it is about the faithful offering and the immediate release.

AGAPE LAB #10: The Resilience Ritual

What do you do with the pain and disappointment after an attempt at connection fails?

If unprocessed, this pain hardens into cynicism, convincing us never to try again.

This lab is a private, contemplative practice — a resilience ritual — designed to help you navigate the aftermath of a collapsed bridge. It guides you through three movements:

1. Lament: honestly name and grieve the loss or failure.
2. Honour: acknowledge your own faithfulness—the courage it took simply to try.
3. Release: prayerfully hand the outcome to God, entrusting the unseen seeds to His care.

This ritual builds the spiritual resilience needed to keep your heart open, even when it hurts.

Reflection On The Blessed Bruising And The Work Ahead

Let us pause and take a breath. The ground we have just crossed in Part III is the most rugged of the entire journey. This section has cost you something. It asked more than reflection; it asked movement, risk, and vulnerability.

You have stepped out of the fortress of certainty into the exposed field of another's story.

You have sat at a table with an IRA member in Belfast and felt the tension of fragile peace.

You have wrestled with the counter-intuitive physics of the Kingdom, where the world's weakness is God's strength. You have walked through the slow, painful process of forgiveness and stood in the lonely ruins of a collapsed bridge.

This work is not clean. It is not simple. To practise Holy Trespass is to accept a certain kind of bruising — to know that you will not always be understood, that your motives will be questioned, and that your efforts will sometimes fail spectacularly. If you have felt that weight, you are on the right path.

This bruising is sacred. The postures of Holy Trespass — sacrificial listening, leading with lament, radical curiosity — are all forms of kenosis, the self-emptying love Christ modelled.

To listen deeply is to empty yourself of the need to be right.

To forgive is to empty yourself of the right to revenge.

To love your enemy is to empty yourself of the ego's need for a caricature to despise.

If we do this honestly, it will break us — our pride, our categories, our craving for tidy outcomes. But this is not a tragic breaking; it is holy breaking. It is the blessed breaking of the bread at the Last Supper — the kind that precedes abundance.

We arrive here bearing our own wounds, the shrapnel from the walls we dared to approach.

And paradoxically, this is exactly where God needs us.

Here lies the secret no one tells you about bridge-building: you cannot build a bridge out of flawless steel. Those bridges are rigid and lifeless. The only authentic bridges are built from the broken pieces of our own lives.

It is only when we have been bruised by the work of love that we can truly connect with a bruised world.

Our failures become our credentials.

Our scars become our entry points.

Our own need for forgiveness is what qualifies us to offer it.

We cannot be healers until we have acknowledged our own wounds.

And that is where we turn now. We have been beautifully broken by the work of love; now we learn the art of holy reconstruction.

The final section of our journey — Part IV — is about just that: building with our broken pieces.

We will explore the gospel according to the Japanese art of kintsugi, where fractured pottery is made more beautiful by filling its cracks with gold.

If Part III was about the breaking, Part IV is about the mending — how God takes the new cracks we earned by trying, forgiving, failing, and loving, and illuminates them with His grace.

We now leave the battlefield of trespass and step into the workshop of the Divine Artisan, who specialises in shattered things. It is time to see how God builds His most beautiful creations not from our strength, but from the radiant, golden seams of our scars.

PART IV:
BUILD BROKEN PIECES

We have come a long way. We have found the courage to see the walls around us, and we have practised the art of trespassing over them. But this work inevitably leaves us with a painful and beautiful truth: we are all, in some way, broken. Our world is broken. Our communities are broken. And our own hearts are broken — by the failures, wounds, and betrayals we have both endured and enacted.

The world tells us to hide our brokenness, to discard what is shattered, to present a smooth, unblemished surface. But the God of the Cross is a God who specialises in broken things.

He is not afraid of our fractures. In fact, the core belief of our faith is that God's greatest work is done not in spite of our brokenness, but through it.

This final section of our journey is about learning to build with those broken pieces.

It is about discovering that our wounds, our failures, and our scars are not shameful liabilities to be hidden, but the very raw materials God uses to build bridges of grace, compassion, and uncommon beauty.

It is time to learn the art of holy reconstruction.

Chapter 11
Beauty in the Cracks

The Gospel According To Kintsugi

There are wounds too deep for stitches, betrayals too complex for justice. But grace does not wait for perfect conditions. It finds the broken edges — and pours in gold.

In the years following the 1994 Rwandan genocide, the nation faced an unbearable question: How do we live again among those who once tried to destroy us?

In response, a radical social and spiritual experiment began — the creation of Reconciliation Villages such as Mbyo and Kigeme, where genocide survivors and perpetrators who had served their sentences were resettled side by side, rebuilding their homes and lives together. It was a theological declaration written in soil and cinder blocks: that God's peace is possible even where blood once ran through the streets.

For Marie Mukamana, it felt less like theology and more like cruel irony.

At nineteen, she had survived the genocide by hiding in a school latrine for four days while her parents and two siblings were hacked to death in her village.

Years later, after the Gacaca courts had done their work and some of the killers were released, Marie was resettled in a new village. By a twist of providence, the man given the plot of land next to hers was Theoneste Habimana — one of the men who had taken part in the murder of her family.

At first, the wall between them was absolute — built of silence as thick as stone.

She avoided eye contact when fetching water, her gaze fixed on the red earth.

He took the long way around her small home to reach the road, eyes downcast in shame.

But village life allows little room for permanent avoidance. Water must be fetched. Roads must be repaired. Food must be grown. Their proximity was a constant, low-grade torture — a daily reopening of an unhealed wound. How could a bridge ever be built across a chasm so wide and so deep?

There is a traditional Japanese art form called kintsugi. When a beloved piece of pottery shatters, the artisan does not discard it. Instead, they gather the fragments, piece them back together, and trace the fault lines with lacquer dusted in powdered gold. The repair is not hidden; it is honoured. The scar becomes the centrepiece. The wound — once a source of shame — becomes the source of the object's unique worth and beauty.

"The place where you are broken is the place where the light gets in."
— *Leonard Cohen*

This, to me, is the most perfect metaphor for the strange and beautiful way God works in the world. Our culture tells us to hide our brokenness — to present a smooth, flawless veneer. But in the Christian story, God's specialty is not mere restoration; it is transfiguration. He does not simply fix what is broken — He makes the broken places the most glorious.

The Apostle Paul is not speaking in abstract poetry when he writes that God, "being rich in mercy… made us alive with Christ," even when we "were dead" in our brokenness.

He is describing what Jesus is — the gold between fractured people, the healing seam, the joining agent who fills the divide with Himself.

I have seen this in my own life. The parts of my story I most wanted to hide — my failures, my losses, my deepest shames — have, over time, become the very places where others have found the most hope. Why? Because scars that shine with the gold of grace are far more trustworthy, far more beautiful, than the illusion of a flawless life.

Kintsugi reminds us of a profound truth: redemption doesn't erase our cracks; it redeems them, honours them, and illuminates them with love. When the Church is most truthful, it is not a museum of perfect, unbroken vessels — it is a community of golden seams.

"God can make beautiful things out of dust — even more so out of a cracked heart."

— Makoto Fujimura

The story of the early Church itself is a story of kintsugi. Its first great fault line emerged between Jewish followers of Jesus and Gentile converts — a collision of cultures, histories, and sacred identities. The Jewish believers insisted the Gentiles must first become Jews — be circumcised, follow dietary laws — before they could truly belong.

It was a wall of hostility built on centuries of tradition.

The conflict threatened to fracture the movement before it ever took root. At the Council of Jerusalem, recorded in Acts, the leaders gathered amid deep tension.

Guided by the Holy Spirit, they made a radical decision: they refused to force the Gentiles to become Jews. They affirmed that faith in Christ alone was the bond that held them together.

In that moment — as Paul would later write to the Ephesians — Jesus Himself became their peace, destroying "the barrier, the dividing wall of hostility," to create "one new humanity out of the two." The Church was born as a kintsugi vessel — a new creation made from shattered fragments, held together by the golden love of Christ.

In the reconciliation village in Rwanda, the first drop of golden lacquer came in the form of an escaped goat. One afternoon, Marie's goat broke free from its pen and became tangled in a wire fence. Theoneste saw it first. He could have ignored it — but he didn't.

He untangled the frightened animal and led it back to her pen. He said nothing, then walked away.

It was a small act. But it was everything. "I saw him differently after that," Marie said later. "He didn't owe me kindness. But he gave it."

The healing, like kintsugi, was slow and deliberate. Through a village-based truth and reconciliation programme, Theoneste eventually offered a full, public confession — detailing his role in the slaughter. Marie stood with her arms folded tightly, tears streaming, as she listened. Weeks later, she began attending the same small prayer gatherings as him. And one day, she offered him forgiveness — not because it erased her pain, but because, as she said, "God forgave me of my own hatred. I had to pass it on."

Now, Marie and Theoneste tend adjoining gardens. They share tools. They co-lead a farming project for the village youth. The crack between them — a chasm once filled with death — has not disappeared. It has been filled with something new.

"We are like a pot that was cracked by fire," Marie says. "But now God has filled the cracks with gold. We are not what we were. We are more."

"Forgiveness is the soil where resurrection grows." — Desmond Tutu

The Rwandan reconciliation villages defy most Western models of post-conflict justice, which prioritise punishment and separation. Rwanda's model, born of necessity, rests on enforced proximity — the belief that shared labour and daily interdependence can cultivate restoration. By compelling former enemies to work side by side — farming, fetching water, repairing roads — these villages create countless small, humanising encounters like the incident with the goat. These simple, sacred gestures become the foundation upon which the harder work of forgiveness can be built.

The spiritual power of Marie's forgiveness is almost blinding. Her words — "God forgave me of my own hatred" — reveal a soul that has wrestled deeply with the Parable of the Unforgiving Servant. She grasped that the grace she had received from God, in being freed from vengeance, was a grace she was now called to extend — no matter how costly. Her forgiveness was not just about Theoneste; it was about her own liberation.

Their shared garden is not merely symbolic — it is a living Eucharist: a patch of soil where life is cultivated where death once reigned. It is a stunning, living piece of Kingdom kintsugi.

And this divine art of repairing with gold is not reserved for the aftermath of genocide.

God practises it quietly — in the hidden ruins of our own failures, marriages, and callings.

Pastor Raymond Lin once embodied success. The celebrated leader of a megachurch in Singapore, his sermons drew thousands; his books sold worldwide. But beneath the polish, Raymond was burning out. He neglected his marriage, micromanaged his staff, and ignored every limit God had placed for his protection. In 2016, it all collapsed.

A series of poor financial decisions — not criminal, but rooted in pride — were leaked to the press. He resigned in shame. His name, once synonymous with spiritual excellence, became a cautionary tale of pastoral failure.

This was his shattering. Raymond moved to a remote town seeking anonymity. He stopped preaching. For two years, he washed dishes in the back of a friend's restaurant. He battled insomnia, depression, and the vertigo of irrelevance. "I thought God had put me on the shelf permanently," he said.

One night, unable to sleep, he opened his Bible and his eyes fell on the words of Isaiah: "He has sent me to bind up the broken-hearted… to give them a crown of beauty instead of ashes." He wept.

From that moment, a new ministry began to form in the ashes of the old. Raymond started leading small retreats for pastors and leaders who were burnt out or broken. He didn't teach; he listened. His own profound brokenness, once his disqualification, became his greatest qualification.

A former attendee wrote, "Raymond didn't try to fix me. He just sat in the ash with me — and pointed to a God who stays."

Today, Raymond runs a spiritual care centre he named Mercy Seam. Its mission is simple: to help other leaders find grace after a great collapse. "Failure didn't end my ministry," he says. "It began it. The pulpit never taught me what the silence of disgrace did. I would not trade the gold in these cracks for all the applause in the world."

Our modern success culture — both in church and corporate life — often creates brittle, inauthentic leaders. We celebrate strength and hide weakness, which breeds the terror of exposure. Pastor Lin's journey models what some thinkers call antifragile leadership — not a system that merely resists shocks, but one that grows stronger through them. By embracing failure and integrating its lessons, Raymond became a more compassionate and resilient leader than he ever was in success. His story proves that our deepest wounds often hold our greatest wisdom.

The art of kintsugi teaches what the Cross has always proclaimed: that what is fractured is not to be discarded; that our wounds can become windows for grace to enter; and that our cracks, filled with the golden love of God, can shine more brightly than the original, unbroken glaze ever could.

Redemption is not a simple repair, returning us to what we were. It is a radical transformation — making us something new. And those who have been cracked but kept walking, who have lost much yet still offer peace, are the most radiant testimonies of God's artistry in a broken world.

FIELD GUIDE:
CHAPTER 11 INTEGRATION

The world tells us to hide what is broken. The God of the Cross specialises in it. Use these tools to begin the practice of seeing your own story not as a list of failures to be concealed, but as a testimony of grace to be illuminated.

1. Theological Meditation Point

Carry this beautiful truth with you this week. Let it be a comfort in moments of shame and a source of hope when you feel inadequate.

My brokenness is not a disqualification from God's love; it is the very canvas upon which He creates His most beautiful art. My scars, when offered to Him, do not need to be hidden — they can become golden seams of grace for the world to see.

2. Questions for Reader Practice

Set aside time for this reflection with a spirit of gentleness and compassion towards yourself. The goal is not to dwell on past pain, but to discover God's redemptive craftsmanship within it.

- The Japanese art of kintsugi honours the break instead of hiding it. What is a "crack" or past failure in your own life that you have consistently tried to conceal out of shame or embarrassment?

- Pastor Raymond Lin's public failure ultimately became the source of his greatest compassion and wisdom. Looking back at the "crack" you just identified, can you see any unexpected "gold" that was forged in that break — a new strength, a deeper empathy, or a wisdom you could not have gained otherwise?
- Marie and Theoneste's shared brokenness, once a wall between them, became the foundation for a new community in their Reconciliation Village. How might the story of your own "golden fracture" become a source of hope or connection for someone else, if you found the courage to share it?

3. Mini-Guide for Daily Embodying: Marking Your Cracks with Gold

Before the deeper work of "The Golden-Fracture Journal," this small, daily practice helps you train your eyes to see the kintsugi process in your everyday life.

Step 1: Identify a Daily "Crack." Each day this week, notice one small moment of brokenness. It doesn't have to be a major failure; it could be a mistake you made at work, a moment when you lost patience with a loved one, or a fleeting sense of inadequacy.

Step 2: Find the Glimmer of Gold. At the end of the day, write down the "crack" in a notebook or journal. Then, next to it, prayerfully identify one piece of "gold" that came from it — or could come from it. For example:

Crack: I was impatient with my children at bedtime.

Gold: It revealed how exhausted I am and reminded me to apologise in the morning — modelling how to repair a relationship.

This practice trains your heart to look for the gold in the cracks of your daily life.

Agape Lab #11: The Golden-Fracture Journal

This lab is a private journaling practice that invites you to become a kintsugi artist of your own story. It is a guided reflection designed to help you look back at a painful experience, a failure, or a "crack" in your life — not to dwell on the pain, but to prayerfully seek the gold within it.

This exercise will provide a series of prompts to help you reframe your narrative:

Where did this crack teach you something you could not have learned otherwise?

What strength, wisdom, or compassion was forged in that very break?

How might God be using that "golden fracture" today as a source of healing and connection for others?

This is not about rewriting history, but about recognising God's redemptive presence within it.

Chapter 12
The God Who Enters the Wound

"The God who was supposed to protect me became the shadow that haunted me."

What happens when the very sanctuary you sought for safety becomes the epicentre of your wounds? When faith fuses with fear, and holiness becomes indistinguishable from harm?

Alina, now in her early forties, lives with a ghost. Not the ghost of her father — the man who was a lay pastor in a Pentecostal church in rural Alberta and a violent predator in his own home — but the ghost of the God he preached about: a God of punishing authority, whose gaze felt like constant, searing surveillance.

A God who demanded obedience and promised protection — a protection that, for Alina, never came.

From the ages of six to fifteen, she endured his sexual abuse — her childhood a landscape of terror and confusion. The same hands that rose to bless the congregation on Sunday were the hands that violated her in the dark. When she finally escaped at seventeen, reported the abuse, and watched in horror as her church rallied around her father, the God she had been taught to fear and appease collapsed into ash. Her first act of freedom was defiance — a declaration forged in the furnace of betrayal: "If God is anything like him, I want nothing to do with Him."

For over a decade, she drifted through a fog of trauma. Panic attacks stole her breath. Periods of dissociation left her watching her own life from a distance. Insomnia turned every night into a sleepless vigil. She tried atheism, but it offered no comfort. She tried yoga, mindfulness, agnosticism —but nothing felt safe. It wasn't faith she had lost, she realised. It was trust — trust in God, in people, and most of all, in her own body, which had become a site of betrayal.

"The soul always remembers the wound that taught it to survive." — Clarissa Pinkola Estés

So many who have endured deep trauma are handed a version of God that is utterly useless in the aftermath. We are given a Triumphant God — a God who fixes, who protects, who wins. But what do you do when that God fails to show up? When the God who was supposed to intervene does not?

That God becomes another source of shame. We are told, implicitly or directly, that if we just had more faith, our wounds would heal — that anxiety would vanish, that the past would lose its grip. We are told to move on. To forgive. To let it go. But trauma doesn't obey commands. And neither, it turns out, does the God of Jesus Christ.

When Jesus appears to His disciples after the resurrection in the Gospel of John, He does not come robed in untouchable glory. He does not appear as a celestial trophy scrubbed clean of pain. He shows up with scars.

Let us sit with that for a moment: the resurrected, glorified, victorious Son of God still bears the holes in His hands. His first act is not to display His power, but to reveal His wounds.

He finds a terrified and doubting Thomas — a man whose trauma from the crucifixion has manifested as a desperate need for proof — and He does not rebuke him.

He invites him closer, into the very heart of His pain.

"Put your finger here; see My hands," Jesus says. "Reach out your hand and put it into My side."

He doesn't say, I've moved on. He doesn't say, It's all in the past. He says, Touch where it hurt.

In this single, stunning act, Jesus dismantles the lie that holiness requires us to hide our wounds.

He does not conceal His trauma in the resurrection — He integrates it.

His wounds become part of His glory, not blemishes upon it.

For anyone who has survived trauma, this is a life-altering revelation:

you do not have to be fully healed to be holy. You do not have to erase your past to walk in the resurrection. God is not ashamed of your scars; He wears His own.

This sacred truth is echoed by what neuroscience now teaches us about trauma.

Trauma is not a story we tell — it is a state our body enters. When we face a threat we cannot escape, the nervous system shifts into survival: fight, flight, or — in its deepest form — freeze and collapse. The residue of that state is trauma: the body continuing to live in threat long after danger has passed.

Healing, therefore, cannot begin with logic or theology alone. As trauma expert Dr. Bessel van der Kolk reminds us, "You can't talk someone out of a trauma response." Healing begins with safety. A dysregulated nervous system must meet a regulated, attuned, safe presence before it can come back online. This is called co-regulation — the quiet miracle of what a mother does when she rocks a crying infant, her steady calm soothing the baby's distress. And this, I believe, is the very work of the Holy Spirit.

In that same scene in John 20, after revealing His wounds, Jesus breathes on the disciples and says, "Receive the Holy Spirit." The breath of God enters their fear-locked room. It is not an overpowering gust, but a gentle, regulating exhale. For bodies trapped in the shallow, panicked breathing of trauma, the slow breath of God is the beginning of peace. The Holy Spirit is not merely an idea to be understood — the Spirit is God's own breath entering our dysregulated bodies, a divine co-regulator who sits with us in our fear until our breathing slows, until our hearts feel safe again.

For Alina, healing began not in a church, but in the quiet circle of a trauma recovery group.

One afternoon, another member read that same passage from John 20. A phrase struck her like a thunderclap she could feel in her bones: "Touch My wounds."

She began to weep uncontrollably. "For the first time," she later said, "I realised Jesus wasn't ashamed of His scars. He didn't gaslight Thomas or scold him for doubt. He simply offered His pain as a place of connection."

That moment became the first thread in a long, slow reweaving of faith.

The image of God as punishing judge began to dissolve, replaced by a new, tender vision: God as the Wounded Companion.

Alina's journey did not end in triumphal resolution. She still lives with Complex Post-Traumatic Stress Disorder (CPTSD). But her body, once a site of terror, has slowly begun to feel safe again. She practises sitting in silence, closing her eyes, imagining the scarred Christ beside her — not saying much, simply staying. Simply breathing.

She found a trauma-informed therapist who integrated Scripture with embodied practices like breathwork and EMDR (Eye Movement Desensitisation and Reprocessing).

Through that work, she began to reclaim the Psalms — not as polished declarations of faith, but as raw prayers of lament she could scream, sob, or whisper.

Eventually, she returned to church — not the Pentecostal congregation of her childhood, but a small Anglican parish rich with silence, liturgy, and candlelight.

"I stopped trying to believe in a God who fixes things from on high," she says.

"I now trust in a God who sits with me in the ashes and whispers, 'Me too.'"

Today, Alina volunteers at a centre for survivors of clerical abuse. She doesn't preach or offer answers. She listens. And sometimes, when sitting with someone in the raw ache of their story, she will quietly share the words that began her own healing:

"Jesus still has His scars, you know. He said, 'Touch My wounds.' If He doesn't need to hide His scars to be whole, then maybe we don't either."

"Jesus doesn't hide His scars; He shows them as a way of saying, 'Me too.'" — Nadia Bolz-Weber

Alina's story is a profound testimony to faith's deconstruction and reconstruction.

For many survivors of religious trauma, the image of God they were given is so entangled with abuse that it must be torn down completely. That tearing down is not the loss of faith — it is its preservation. It is the courageous work of spiritual survival.

The reconstruction that follows is about finding a new, safer, truer image of God.

For Alina, it was the Wounded Christ — not the omnipotent perpetrator of control, but the fellow survivor, whose power is expressed not through domination, but through solidarity in suffering.

The Church has, for too long, offered answers to people who are not asking questions but living in a state of terror. We have offered theology to dysregulated nervous systems.

Alina's journey teaches us that the first gift we must offer the traumatised is not doctrine, but presence — a regulated, safe, non-anxious presence. We are called to be the body of Christ, and in this context, that means becoming a collective nervous system for one another: a community that can hold pain, breathe with the grieving, and wait — patiently, tenderly — until someone feels safe enough to believe again in the possibility of a God who is love.

"We need communities that don't rush to heal us but dare to sit beside us as we bleed."

— Kate Bowler

This need for collective safety extends far beyond individual trauma. It is the same need that arises in the wake of the tragedies that shatter entire communities.

In 2012, a gunman entered Sandy Hook Elementary School in Newtown, Connecticut, killing twenty children and six adults. The trauma did not remain confined to the families of the victims — it seeped into the soil of the town itself. Grief became the new atmosphere.

Children across Newtown developed phobias of loud noises. Parents suffered panic attacks in the aisles of the supermarket. Teachers found themselves unable to re-enter classrooms without reliving the horror in their bodies. It was not simply a mental health crisis — it was a physiological one.

What followed was not a tidy "healing process," but a communal nervous system response.

Trauma-informed counsellors were embedded in schools, firehouses, and churches.

Faith communities gathered for interfaith vigils where the goal was not to explain, but to weep together. Parents formed remembrance circles that expressed grief through action — painting benches, planting trees, reading poetry in silence. Local yoga teachers and therapists offered free somatic sessions at the town hall, creating spaces where grieving bodies could breathe, shake, move, and cry.

This was the community becoming its own body — a collective nervous system learning to regulate together. From that shared grief, something astonishing emerged: The Sandy Hook Promise, an advocacy movement founded by the victims' families to prevent gun violence.

Their grief became agency.

"We didn't move on from our grief," one father said. "We learned to move with it — together."

Newtown remains a town marked by sacred scars. But its deep pain has become a golden seam — a place of witness to what can be forged when love holds grief without rushing it away.

The response in Newtown stands as a model of trauma-informed community care.

In the face of mass tragedy, the instinct is often to offer "thoughts and prayers" from afar.

But Newtown shows that true healing requires proximity, presence, and practical, embodied care. Before they could advocate for policy change, they first had to create spaces where their nervous systems could feel safe again. Their journey from collective grief to collective action reveals that social transformation often begins not in ideology, but in the shared experience of a wound that refuses to be ignored.

Trauma does not vanish in the light of faith. But in the light of a boundaryless, trespassing God, neither does our trauma go untouched.

The resurrected Christ appears not as a sanitised icon of perfection, but as a scarred Saviour, holding out His hands and saying,

"Put your hands here. See where it hurt."

And in that touch — that raw, trembling moment of shared vulnerability — healing begins.

This is our deepest hope: that God does not wait for us to climb out of the pit of our pain.

God descends into it with us, sits beside us in the dark, breathes with us until our breath returns, and whispers:

"You are not broken beyond repair. You are beloved in your fragments."

We are not only harmed by what was done to us; we are also haunted by what it taught us to believe. In the next chapter, we descend into that haunted place — the maze of internalised shame — where the adversary is not another person, but the voice in our own head.

FIELD GUIDE: CHAPTER 12 INTEGRATION

The journey of healing from trauma is slow, sacred, and deeply personal. It is a path we walk one breath at a time. Use these tools this week to practise finding the safe, regulating presence of the Wounded God in your own body and your own story.

1. Theological Meditation Point

Carry this radical truth with you. Let it be a gentle counter-voice to any shame that tells you must be "fixed" to be worthy of God's presence.

God does not wait for me to be healed before He draws near. He meets me in the wound itself, offering His own scars as a point of connection, and His gentle presence as a place of safety for my soul and my body.

2. Questions for Reader Practice

Set aside quiet time for this reflection. Approach these questions with the same tenderness and compassion that God has for you.

- Alina's healing began when her image of God shifted from a Punishing Judge to a Wounded Companion. What is the primary image of God you hold when you are in pain or distress? Is it a God who is distant and demanding, or one who is near, wounded, and present?

- This chapter suggests that trauma is stored in the body. Where in your own body do you tend to feel stress, fear, or the memory of past pain? (e.g. a tight chest, a clenched jaw, a knot in your stomach).
- Jesus appears to His disciples with His resurrection scars, showing that wounds can be integrated into a new, whole life. What would it mean for you to believe that your own scars do not need to be hidden to be holy, but can become part of your story of resurrection?

3. Mini-Guide for Daily Embodying: The Safe Space Anchor

Before engaging in the deeper work of the "Breath Prayer," this small practice helps you connect the theological idea of God's presence to the physical sensations of safety in your body.

Step 1: Identify a Sensation of Safety. Find one small thing in your immediate physical environment that makes you feel even a little safe or calm. It could be the weight of a blanket on your lap, the warmth of a cup of tea in your hands, the sight of a tree outside your window, or the sound of gentle music.

Step 2: Connect Presence to Sensation. Once a day, take 60 seconds to focus entirely on that physical sensation. As you feel the warmth or notice the colour, connect that feeling of safety to the idea of God as a quiet, co-regulating presence. You might whisper a simple phrase such as, "God, you are this warmth," or "Holy Spirit, you are this quiet."

The practice is to train your body — not just your mind — to recognise that God's presence can be found in the tangible, sensory details of the present moment.

AGAPE LAB #12: Meeting God in the Nervous System — A Breath Prayer for the Traumatised Soul

This is not a lab about thinking; it is a lab about breathing. For those who have experienced trauma, the body often exists in a state of high alert, and prayer can feel impossible when your nervous system is screaming "danger."

This guided practice offers a gentle, embodied way to connect with the safe, regulating presence of the Holy Spirit. Using a simple breath prayer synchronised with the rhythm of your own breathing — for example, breathing in "Holy Spirit," and breathing out "Be my peace" — this exercise guides you to notice the sensations in your body and to invite the gentle, non-anxious presence of God into those very places.

It is a way to practise receiving the divine exhale of the Spirit, allowing your body — not just your mind — to experience the truth that you are safe and held in this very moment.

Chapter 13
From Echo Chamber to Sanctuary

Forging A Boundaryless Community

Some walls are made of brick. Others are built from silence, suspicion, and the stories we refuse to hear. To tear them down, we need more than good intentions — we need tables, questions, and the courage to stay.

In Portland's King neighbourhood, you can see the wall without even looking for it.

It's a line that runs invisibly down the middle of the street, yet everyone feels it.

On one side lies the old King — the historically Black community that has called it home for generations. Its anchor is a corner barbershop, the heartbeat of the block, where, as one resident recalls, "the laughter used to be loud on these porches." On the other side is the new King — a product of Portland's rapid gentrification. Its anchor is a minimalist coffee shop serving single-origin pour-overs to the young, mostly white professionals, artists, and tech workers who have moved into renovated bungalows and sleek condos.

The divide isn't just aesthetic; it's economic, racial, and generational. Longtime residents — Black families, ageing renters, immigrants — feel their culture, history, and even existence being erased by rising rents and an influx of polite but detached new neighbours. The newcomers, meanwhile, carry a mixture of awkward guilt and genuine desire to connect — but often have no idea how. Tension bubbles up at city council meetings over zoning, policing, and the ever-present threat of eviction.

Into this fractured landscape, a multi-ethnic, faith-rooted community called The Table Collective opened its doors — right on the fault line between the old and the new.

Their mission was not to pick a side, but something far harder: to build a sanctuary in a neighbourhood at war with itself.

The human longing for sanctuary is primal. We all ache for a place where we are safe, known, and loved. Yet too often, what we build is not a sanctuary at all, but its counterfeit — an echo chamber.

An echo chamber is a space where sameness is policed. It feels safe because it is predictable.

Everyone looks, thinks, and votes like you. Its function is to reinforce what its members already believe, shielding them from the discomfort of difference. It cannot hold pain. It cannot hold paradox.

"A safe space is not where we are protected from the truth, but where the truth is welcomed without fear." — bell hooks

A sanctuary, on the other hand, is something braver. It is a space where difference doesn't threaten belonging; where questions are welcome, wounds are not hidden, and truth can be spoken without being weaponised.

Theologically, an echo chamber is built on fear disguised as certainty. A sanctuary is built on love — a love wide enough to welcome the stranger, including the strange and wounded parts of ourselves.

A true sanctuary says, with its open doors: You don't have to be like me to be loved by me.

"Hospitality means we take people into the space that is our lives and our minds and our hearts and our work and our efforts. Hospitality is not to change people, but to offer them space where change can take place." — Henri Nouwen

The early church, as described in the Book of Acts, is often romanticised as a utopian community.

But look closer, and you see something far more powerful — and far more human a porous, Spirit-led, often messy gathering of people who didn't agree on everything, but who chose to stay anyway.

The first followers of Jesus were a motley crew — fishermen, tax collectors, political zealots, and devout women. After the Spirit was poured out at Pentecost, this diversity wasn't erased; it was amplified, creating a multilingual, multi-ethnic community from the beginning.

What bound them together was not doctrinal precision or cultural sameness, but a shared rhythm of grace:

"They devoted themselves to the apostles' teaching and to fellowship, to the breaking of bread and to prayer… All the believers were together and had everything in common. They sold property and possessions to give to anyone who had need."

Their boundaries were radically porous. The line between mine and yours blurred beneath a love that saw a neighbour's need as its own. Their power came not from agreement, but from surrender — to a gospel of grace large enough to hold them all. This is the blueprint for sanctuary.

Consider the story of Ananias and Sapphira in Acts 5. It is a harsh and unsettling story, often misread as divine punishment for withholding money. But their sin was not keeping part of their wealth; it was lying about it. They performed generosity while clinging to control. They wanted the appearance of belonging without the cost of vulnerability — the social benefits of sanctuary while maintaining the safety of an echo chamber. Their story stands as a warning: you cannot have both.

A true sanctuary demands honesty and vulnerability — qualities terrifying to the ego but liberating to the soul.

The leaders of The Table Collective understood this. To build a sanctuary, they had to move beyond talking about community and begin embodying it. Instead of choosing sides — long-time residents or newcomers — they began the slow, sacred work of creating a space that could hold both.

Each month, they hosted a Shared Table Potluck in the church's side yard — a simple act of what they called Dinner Table Diplomacy. Everyone was invited to bring a dish from their heritage. The tables overflowed with collard greens and mac and cheese, vegan quinoa salads, and gluten-free sourdough. No microphones. No speeches. Just name tags, picnic benches, and question cards designed to move conversation past small talk:

"What's one thing you miss about how your neighbourhood used to be?" "What would make you feel more at home here?"

At one of the first dinners, Mr Hughes, an 81-year-old Black man who had lived on the same block for sixty years, was paired with Lexi, a 28-year-old white freelance designer who had moved in six months earlier. When she asked what he missed most, his answer was swift, steeped in longing:

"Laughter," he said, his voice raspy." "Before this block got all quiet and polite. We used to laugh loud on these porches — kids playing, music everywhere. It felt alive."

Lexi, who had moved there for its "quiet, artistic vibe," wept softly into her napkin.

That night, she signed up to volunteer — her idea: a series of free front-porch concerts to bring music and laughter back to the block.

The work deepened when the city proposed rezoning several blocks for high-density development, igniting fears of mass eviction. The Table Collective hosted a town forum — but instead of a contentious debate, they structured it around Sacrificial Listening.

They formed listening circles led by trained mediators. For the first hour, one group spoke while the other only listened. A Somali woman described the terror of receiving an eviction notice after her landlord sold her building. A young white landlord admitted, with shame, that he didn't even know what Section 8 housing was. A lifelong homeowner wept as he confessed his fear that his children would never afford to live in the neighbourhood where they were born. No one yelled. No one interrupted. Everyone listened. The Table Collective didn't solve gentrification. But it built a sanctuary within it. And from that sanctuary, new things began to grow.

A community garden was planted on an abandoned lot, tended by elders, teens, and new arrivals alike. An anti-eviction network emerged, connecting tenants at risk with pro-bono legal aid from local lawyers. And Mr Hughes — with Lexi's help — now leads monthly porch storytelling nights, his laughter once again echoing down the block.

"I still don't agree with everyone here," one resident said after a potluck, "but now I know who they are — their stories. That changed everything."

The Table Collective's approach is a living example of what community organisers call asset-based community development. Rather than seeing a neighbourhood only through the lens of its problems, this method begins by recognising its existing strengths: the wisdom of elders like Mr Hughes, the energy and creativity of newcomers like Lexi, and the shared love for place and people.

The Table didn't act as a charity swooping in to fix the neighbourhood. It acted as a catalyst — creating what sociologist Ray Oldenburg described as a "third space": a neutral, welcoming environment outside of home and work where people from different tribes could build relationships, discover shared assets, and co-create solutions.

The work of The Table Collective is, in many ways, a modern reimagining of the church in Acts 2. Their potlucks became a form of breaking bread. Their listening circles became communal prayer. Their anti-eviction network ensured that, in their own way, "all had everything in common." They understood that the church is not a fortress for hiding from conflict, but a training ground for grace — a place where we develop the muscles to meet disagreement with courage, compassion, and love that transcends our boundaries.

This transformation — from echo chamber to sanctuary — is not just the work of churches or neighbourhoods. It is the urgent work required within our families.

The Ramirez family of San Antonio, Texas, was close-knit and lively — until the 2016 U.S. presidential election split them open. Carlos, the youngest son, was a recent college graduate and an outspoken progressive. His uncle, Tío Miguel, a proud veteran and lifelong conservative, was equally vocal in his defence of Trump.

Thanksgiving that year ended in shouting. Miguel stormed out, shouting, "I don't even know this family anymore!" The aftermath lasted three years. Birthdays were awkward. The group chat fell silent. Every conversation became a minefield of caution and resentment.

In 2020, weary of the distance, Carlos decided to practise what he'd begun reading about — boundary-dissolving curiosity. He called his uncle, not to argue, but to ask a question:

"Tío, I know we disagree on everything right now. But could you tell me a story that shaped your politics — not something you saw on the news, but something from your life?"

Miguel hesitated. Then, slowly began to speak. He told Carlos about his first army deployment — how his faith in American values was forged under fire. Carlos didn't argue. He didn't analyse. He just listened. When his uncle finished, he said softly,

"Thanks for trusting me with that, Tío."

That Christmas, Carlos handed Miguel a letter — an apology not for his politics, but for making his uncle feel unseen in his own family. Miguel wept. They talked for hours. They still disagreed on almost everything, but something had shifted.

Now, every Ramirez gathering begins with a new family rule — one they wrote together:

"We don't argue headlines. We tell stories."

The Ramirez home is no longer an echo chamber. It's a sanctuary with scars — but a sanctuary nonetheless. As Carlos put it, "We stopped trying to win the argument. We just started trying to stay in the room together."

"Community is the fruit of our capacity to make the interests of others more important than our own." — Jean Vanier

Political polarisation works like a destructive feedback loop, especially within families.

Each side creates a caricature of the other, and every encounter reinforces it.

Carlos's question broke that loop. By shifting the focus from positions (which can be debated) to stories (which can only be shared), he humanised the conflict. He didn't try to change his uncle's mind — he tried to understand his uncle's heart.

This is a crucial principle of de-escalation — one that applies everywhere: in marriages, workplaces, and boardrooms. In an age of curated feeds and ideological tribes, the simple act of building a sanctuary is radically countercultural.

The early church didn't change the world through preaching alone. It changed the world by staying at the table — by sharing bread, telling the truth, caring for the needy, and refusing to walk away.

And so, this is your call as a Boundary Dissolver: Build spaces where disagreement doesn't mean exile. Open your door, your table, your heart — especially to the kind of other that makes you uncomfortable. Measure your success not by agreement, but by the quality of your courageous, loving presence.

Because a sanctuary is not a place where everyone is the same. It is a place where everyone is finally safe enough to be known.

Sanctuaries don't protect us from discomfort — they teach us how to hold it with grace.

In the next chapter, we face the final frontier of otherness: loving the ones we swore we never could.

FIELD GUIDE:
CHAPTER 13 INTEGRATION

Building a sanctuary is not the job of a pastor or leader alone; it is the daily, moment-by-moment work of every member of a community. Use these tools this week to begin cultivating a spirit of sanctuary within your own spheres of influence.

1. Theological Meditation Point

Carry this vital distinction with you into your community life this week. Let it challenge and inspire you.

An echo chamber is a space where I feel safe because everyone agrees with me.

A sanctuary is a space where I am safe enough to be known, even in my disagreements.

God does not call me to build a soundproof box of sameness, but sanctuaries of belonging.

2. Questions for Reader Practice

Set aside time to prayerfully consider the communities you are part of. The goal is to see, with new eyes, the places where walls might be forming — and where gates might be opened.

- Think of an important community in your life (your church, workplace, or friendship group). Is it functioning more like an echo chamber, where sameness is policed, or a sanctuary, where difference is welcome? What specific signs do you see?
- The Ramirez family began to heal when Carlos chose to ask a new kind of question and apologise for his part in the conflict. In your own community, what is one way you personally contribute to it being a soundproof box (e.g. avoiding difficult topics, making assumptions, using judgemental language)? What is one small thing you could do to help it become more of a sanctuary?
- The Table Collective intentionally created spaces for newcomers and longtime residents to connect. Who are the "newcomers" or "outsiders" in your community? What do you imagine their experience might be like? What is one step you could take this month to make that space safer or more welcoming for them?

3. Mini-Guide for Daily Embodying: The Sanctuary Minute

Before you attempt a full "Community Temperature Check," this small practice will help you build the core habit of creating sanctuary — one person at a time.

•**Step 1:** Identify One Person. This week, prayerfully identify one person in one of your communities who you sense might feel on the margins — unheard or misunderstood.

Step 2: Create a "Sanctuary Minute." Your task is to intentionally create a 60-second sanctuary for them. This means finding a moment to give your full, undivided, non-judgemental attention. It could be asking a question and practising sacrificial listening without interrupting. It could be publicly affirming something wise they said in a meeting. It could even be simply making eye contact from across the room and offering a genuine smile.

The goal is not to fix their problems, but to use one minute of your day to communicate the core message of sanctuary: "I see you, and you are safe to be yourself here."

AGAPE LAB #13: The Community Temperature Check

This lab is a diagnostic tool to help you prayerfully assess the health of a community you belong to — whether your church, workplace, small group, or family. It is a checklist of questions designed to help you discern whether your community functions more like a protective, fear-based echo chamber or a brave, love-based sanctuary.

The questions will prompt you to reflect on things such as:

- How does our community handle disagreement?
- Who feels least safe or heard here?
- How do we welcome newcomers who are different from us?

The goal is not to produce a score or a verdict, but to identify one small, concrete step you can take to help your community become a more welcoming, grace-filled, and boundary-dissolving space.

Chapter 14
The Last Enemy is a Mirror

Loving The Other In An Age Of Outrage

The hardest boundary to cross is not national or political — it is personal.

It is the invisible line we draw to protect ourselves from the enemy we've fashioned out of our pain. But what if healing doesn't begin with winning, but with weeping together?

Robi Damelin described her grief as a fire that consumed everything.

In 2002, her 28-year-old son, David — a soldier in the Israeli Defence Forces — was killed by a Palestinian sniper. The pain was total, searing, absolute. It hardened quickly into a single, clarifying desire.

"I didn't want to meet 'the other side,'" she would later recall. "I wanted justice. I wanted revenge."

Her grief had found an enemy — a target for its unbearable force — and that enemy became an entire people. This is the tragic logic of sorrow in a divided world: it seeks a focus for its rage, a face to blame for its loss.

Across the wall, in the occupied territories, Bassam Aramin, a former Palestinian resistance fighter, was living a mirror image of her anguish.

In 2007, his ten-year-old daughter, Abir, was shot in the head by an Israeli border police officer while walking home from school. She died in his arms. His loss, too, was absolute. His grief, too, was a consuming fire. He had every reason to build an unbreachable wall of hatred around his heart.

Two parents — an Israeli mother and a Palestinian father — united by the worst kind of intimacy. They could have remained sealed within their fortresses of rage forever,

their stories fuelling the very cycle that had devoured their children.

But instead, they chose the unthinkable. They trespassed across the highest and bloodiest of boundaries. They chose to weep together — and then, astonishingly, to work together.

Their journey began with an invitation to a meeting of the Parents Circle–Families Forum — an organisation of over six hundred bereaved Israeli and Palestinian families who have each lost an immediate relative to the conflict. Robi was sceptical, even hostile. But then someone at the organisation asked her a question that pierced her armour of rage: "Would you prefer to be right, or to be healed?"

"Justice can heal the wound, but only mercy can touch the scar." — Miroslav Volf

That question — Would you prefer to be right, or to be healed? — is the narrow gate into Jesus's hardest command. When He stands before the crowd on the hillside and says, "Love your enemies and pray for those who persecute you," He is not offering sentimental advice for the spiritually elite. He is redefining what it means to be truly human — to reflect the image of a God without borders, a God whose love trespasses even into enemy territory. He immediately follows it with a piercing question of His own: "If you love those who love you, what reward will you get?"

This is not divine idealism. It is divine realism. Jesus is not pretending that enemies do not exist, nor asking us to ignore wounds or abandon justice. He is commanding us to love as God loves — and God's love is recklessly, scandalously impartial.

"He causes His sun to rise on the evil and the good, and sends rain on the righteous and the unrighteous." God's love is not a reward for good behaviour; it is the very pulse of creation —

poured out on everyone, everywhere, without condition. To love our enemy is to align our hearts with that creative pulse.

The act of creating an enemy is the ego's favourite and most efficient shortcut to self-definition.

We construct our identity by contrast: I am not them. I am good because they are bad. I am right because they are wrong. This process of othering is ancient, even adaptive — it forms tribes, offers safety. But theologically, it is profoundly anti-Christ. It is the primal lie of separation — the very illusion Jesus came to dismantle.

He is not merely asking us to be polite to those we dislike. He is inviting us to deconstruct the entire scaffolding of fear and superiority upon which we have built our false selves. In a very real sense, to love your enemy is to finally love the last, rejected part of yourself you have refused to face.

This is the ultimate holy trespass — crossing the final boundary: the one that runs straight through the human heart.

"You do not destroy your enemy when you defeat him. You destroy your enemy when you make him your friend." — Abraham Lincoln

Return now to the Sermon on the Mount. Picture the scene: a crowd gathered under Roman occupation. Their "enemies" were not abstract figures debated on screens;

they were the soldiers patrolling their streets — men who could strike, insult, or compel them to carry their armour for a mile.

In this world, the old law — "an eye for an eye" — was not cruelty. It was justice. It was dignity.

And into that world, Jesus spoke words that must have sounded like madness, even betrayal: "If anyone slaps you on the right cheek, turn to them the other also."

This was not submission. It was subversion. In that culture, a slap on the right cheek was a backhanded blow — a gesture of superiority. To turn the other cheek was to face your oppressor as an equal, to refuse humiliation on their terms.

"If anyone wants to sue you and take your shirt, hand over your coat as well."

In a society where public nakedness shamed the stripper, not the stripped, this was an act of prophetic protest — exposing injustice by revealing the oppressor's moral poverty.

"If anyone forces you to go one mile, go with them two." Roman law permitted soldiers to conscript civilians for exactly one mile. By walking a second, you reclaimed your agency. The first mile is coercion; the second mile is freedom.

Each command reveals a spiritual physics: Jesus is not teaching passivity.

He is showing us a power that does not mirror evil but unmasks it — a power strong enough to transform the world.

The room where Robi and Bassam first met was small, silent, and heavy with the gravity of unspeakable loss. When Robi saw him — this man whose calm presence carried both sorrow and strength — something in her armour began to give way. Her voice trembled as she asked, "How can you sit here after all you've lost?"

His answer came not from ideology, but from the broken, defiant heart of a father:

"Because," he said, looking straight at her, "I refuse to let hatred kill another child — yours or mine."

With those words, the wall between them collapsed. They wept — not as an Israeli and a Palestinian, but as two parents bound by the same sacred, unbearable ache.

Today, Robi Damelin and Bassam Aramin travel the world together as co-spokespersons for the Parents Circle–Families Forum, speaking to schools, parliaments, and communities trapped in their own cycles of vengeance.

Their work is not a utopian dream; it is a living parable — proof that even in the world's most intractable conflicts, the love that dares to cross enemy lines still holds the power to resurrect what hate has buried.

They do not agree on everything. They do not share the same historical narrative or political solution. But they agree on one unshakeable truth. As they often say: "We are no longer enemies. We are bereaved parents. We are family."

Their shared testimony is often met with disbelief, sometimes with anger — but always with awe. Not because their story makes sense in a world of walls, but because, in the end, it is the only thing that ever will.

The work of the Parents Circle is a profound embodiment of what peacebuilders call narrative empathy. The cycle of generational violence runs on a simple, powerful script: We are the victims; they are the perpetrators. That story, told long enough, becomes unquestionable truth.

The genius of the Parents Circle is that it creates a space where those competing narratives are interrupted by a deeper, shared one — the story of grief. By forming a new identity — bereaved parent — that transcends "Israeli" and "Palestinian," they carve out a third space where new stories can begin. They are not erasing the old narratives; they are writing a new one — together.

The journey of Robi and Bassam is a living embodiment of the Cross. Each has taken the unbearable pain of their own crucifixion and refused to turn it into a weapon.

Instead, they have allowed it to become a bridge. This is resurrection power — the mysterious divine alchemy that transforms the worst thing that can happen into a source of life for others. Their work is not sentimental; it is warfare — a spiritual defiance against the principalities of hatred and revenge that hold our world captive.

They are living proof that the blood of their children does not have to be the last word.

"Blessed are the peacemakers, for they shall be called the children of God." — Matthew 5:9

While few of us will ever be called to the heroic work of Robi and Bassam, all of us are called to the same practice — to the daily, domestic work of peace in the culture wars of our own lives.

Ben, a 42-year-old evangelical Christian from rural Ohio, knew the tightness in his stomach each time he saw Congresswoman **Alexandria Ocasio-Cortez on television.**

To him, she embodied everything he feared: radical progressivism, disdain for tradition, and a perceived threat to his religious freedom. He would shout at the screen. He would forward memes. He laughed at cruel jokes made at her expense. He never called it hatred — he called it discernment.

Then one Sunday, his pastor preached on Matthew 5:44: "Pray for those who persecute you."

He had heard it a hundred times. But that morning, the words landed like an accusation — or an invitation. Ben went home in silence, realising with a jolt that he could not imagine her as a human being. She was only a threat, a caricature, an enemy.

So, he began small — a daily act of holy trespass against his own contempt.

Every morning, he prayed: "God, bless Alexandria. Show her Your love. And help me see her through Your eyes."

It felt mechanical at first. Forced. Hollow. But he kept going.

One afternoon, he stumbled across a long interview where she spoke not of policy but of her father's death — of working as a bartender to support her family, of fear and exhaustion. He still disagreed with her politics. But something in him softened. That night, he wrote in his journal: "She is not the enemy. My fear is the enemy."

Ben now teaches a Sunday School class called Conviction Without Contempt. He invites his students to disagree passionately — but to love one another more loudly than they disagree. His politics haven't changed, but his heart has.

"I'm not praying for her to lose anymore," he says. "I'm praying for her to be loved. And I guess that has to include me."

Ben's story is a practical parable of what it means to rehumanise our political opponents.

Modern media — especially the algorithmic echo chambers we explored in Chapter 3 — thrives on flattening our opponents into two-dimensional caricatures. This dehumanisation is the precondition for contempt.

Ben's disciplined practice — praying for his "enemy" and seeking out her human story — was an act of spiritual resistance against this outrage machine. He chose complexity over simplicity, empathy over algorithm, and in doing so, reclaimed his own spiritual agency.

To love our enemy is not to betray our convictions or abandon justice. It is to become like Jesus — to recognise that the true enemy is never the human being before us, but hatred itself: division, fear, the ancient lie of separation.

When you choose to love your enemy, you reclaim your own humanity from the prison of your righteousness. You rob hatred of its most potent weapon — its ability to make you resemble it.

You become a living, breathing sign of the Kingdom of God in a world that has forgotten what love looks like.

As Paul wrote,

"While we were still enemies, Christ died for us."

We are all the enemy God chose to love first.

Adversaries can be disarmed. But mirrors — they reflect what we've buried.

In the next chapter, we face the hidden grief beneath our fiercest convictions — and the surprising grace that waits in the ashes.

FIELD GUIDE:
CHAPTER 14 INTEGRATION

You have reached the summit. The command to love our enemies is not the end of the journey, but the beginning of a new way of life. It is the daily practice of choosing resurrection over resentment. Use these final tools to begin this difficult, beautiful, and world-changing work.

1. Theological Meditation Point

Carry this final, challenging truth with you. Let it be both the mirror in which you examine your own heart and the compass that guides your most difficult relationships.

My adversary is not the person I disagree with; my true enemy is the hate, fear, and division within my own heart. To love my adversary is to engage in the final act of spiritual warfare against that inner darkness, reclaiming my own humanity in the process.

2. Questions for Reader Practice

This last reflection requires radical honesty. Sit with these questions without judgement, simply allowing them to reveal the state of your heart.

- Who is your "enemy"? Be honest. It may not be a single person, but a group, a political party, or an ideology. As Ben did with

AOC, name the face or the idea that tightens your stomach and fuels your contempt.

- The chapter suggests that creating an adversary is the ego's favourite shortcut to self-definition ("I am good because they are bad"). What do you gain from having this enemy? Does it make you feel more certain, more righteous, or more connected to your own tribe?
- Robi and Bassam had to absorb the unimaginable pain of their children's deaths to find a new way forward. What pain, fear, or grievance would you have to be willing to absorb to take the first step towards loving the adversary in your own life?

3. Mini-Guide for Daily Embodying: A Prayer for Your Enemy

Before beginning the deeper, ongoing work of "The Enemy Examen," this small, disciplined practice models the first step Ben took on his journey from contempt to compassion.

Step 1: Commit to One Minute. For the next seven days, commit to a one-minute daily practice. Recall the specific enemy you identified in the reflection questions. Acknowledge the anger or contempt you feel — do not attempt to suppress it.

Step 2: Pray Ben's Prayer. Take one deep breath, and pray Ben's simple, difficult prayer for them: "God, bless [their name]. Show them Your love. And please, help me see them through Your eyes." It will likely feel forced or even hypocritical at first — just as it did for Ben. That is okay. The practice is not about manufacturing a feeling. It is a rugged act of will, a small trespass against the threshold of your own heart that, over time, allows the grace of a boundaryless God to begin its transformative work.

AGAPE LAB #14: The "Enemy" Examen

This final lab is a private and courageous inventory of the heart. It is a guided reflection based on the traditional Examen, but focused specifically on the adversary in your own life.

It will invite you to identify the person, group, or political figure you have cast in this role, then guide you through a series of prompts — not to change your mind about important issues, but to begin the difficult work that Ben undertook.

It will help you move from a prayer about them to a prayer for them.

This structured practice leads you to take one small, difficult step from contempt towards compassionate opposition, asking God to help you see even your adversary through His boundaryless eyes.

Epilogue: The Demolition Continues

The last page of a book is a dangerous place. It's tempting to close the cover and feel a sense of completion. It's tempting to mistake the feeling of finishing the book for the feeling of finishing the work.

Let's be honest — just as we were in the introduction. The work is not finished. In fact, it has just begun.

You can already feel it, can't you? The mortar is still wet on the new walls the world is building. Tomorrow, the algorithm will hand you a brick. The news cycle will offer you a trowel. Your own comfort will beg you to find the old, familiar blueprints for the echo chamber you used to live in. The temptation to rebuild will be overwhelming.

This book was never meant to be a map to a boundaryless place. It was an invitation to become a boundaryless person.

And here is the good, terrifying news: the Wrecking Ball is still in your hand.

The four pillars we walked through are not a one-time construction project; they are a daily, rugged practice.

- You will need to receive the demolition of God's love again and again, especially when you find yourself hiding behind new walls of certainty or self-righteousness.

- You will need to see the invisible fences every morning, recognising the new ways fear and tribalism are trying to shrink your heart.
- You will need to practise holy trespass in small, costly ways—in the comment section, across the holiday table, and in the quiet of your own prayers (especially the Enemy Examen).
- And you will need to build with broken pieces, resisting the urge to find perfect people and instead choosing to create a sanctuary with the real, messy, and beautifully fractured people God has put in your life.

The Boundaryless God did not just break down a wall for you. He is breaking down the walls within you, so He can continue His wall-breaking work through you.

This work is not comfortable. It is not efficient. It will not win you fans in a divided world. It is the slow, holy, and often hidden work of un-building. It is the art of subtraction. It is the ministry of becoming smaller, more open, and more available to the "other."

Do not be afraid. You are not building a fortress. You are being rebuilt as a bridge.

Now, go. The demolition continues.

Bibliography

Boyle, Gregory. Tattoos on the Heart: The Power of Boundless Compassion. New York: Free Press, 2010.

Cone, James H. The Cross and the Lynching Tree. Maryknoll, NY: Orbis Books, 2011.

Lewis, C. S. The Four Loves. London: Geoffrey Bles, 1960.

Moltmann, Jürgen. The Crucified God: The Cross of Christ as the Foundation and Criticism of Christian Theology. Translated by R. A. Wilson and John Bowden. Minneapolis: Fortress Press, 1993.

Nouwen, Henri J. M. Reaching Out: The Three Movements of the Spiritual Life. New York: Doubleday, 1975.

Nygren, Anders. Agape and Eros. Translated by Philip S. Watson. Chicago: University of Chicago Press, 1982.

Palmer, Parker J. Healing the Heart of Democracy: The Courage to Create a Politics Worthy of the Human Spirit. San Francisco: Jossey-Bass, 2011.

Pariser, Eli. The Filter Bubble: What the Internet Is Hiding from You. New York: Penguin Press, 2011.

Rohr, Richard. The Universal Christ: How a Forgotten Reality Can Change Everything We See, Hope For, and Believe. New York: Convergent Books, 2019.

Sunstein, Cass R. #Republic: Divided Democracy in the Age of Social Media. Princeton: Princeton University Press, 2017.

Turkle, Sherry. Reclaiming Conversation: The Power of Talk in a Digital Age. New York: Penguin Press, 2015.

Tutu, Desmond, and Mpho Tutu. The Book of Forgiving: The Fourfold Path for Healing Ourselves and Our World. New York: HarperOne, 2014.

Volf, Miroslav. Exclusion and Embrace: A Theological Exploration of Identity, Otherness, and Reconciliation. Nashville: Abingdon Press, 1996.

Zuboff, Shoshana. The Age of Surveillance Capitalism: The Fight for a Human Future at the New Frontier of Power. New York: PublicAffairs, 2019.

About the Author

Stephen Fuka Feka is a Catholic priest, writer, and teacher serving in the Democratic Republic of Congo. It is from this frontline, at the intersection of profound faith, human conflict, and deep-seated division, that he writes *The Boundaryless God*.

Stephen's message is not one of abstract theology but of costly, lived experience. His own ministry was forged in a moment of profound personal failure on the mission field, an experience he shares in the book, which became the "divine wrecking ball" that tore down his own walls and taught him the true nature of God's relentless, boundary-breaking love.

A missionary priest ordained in 2018, he has served as a parish priest, formator, and builder of sanctuaries. His work is informed by rigorous academic study, holding distinctions in both Philosophy and Theology from his formation in Cameroon, where he also served as editor of the seminary's Search Light magazine.

This powerful combination of rigorous study and raw, on-the-ground ministry gives Stephen a unique voice to challenge the "invisible fences" and "sacred cows" that divide our world. He is passionate about guiding others to practice the "holy trespass" of forgiveness, curiosity, and the art of building new, more beautiful communities from our broken pieces.

Today, he serves as a parish priest where, in addition to his pastoral duties, he embodies the boundaryless love he writes about by supporting over two dozen vulnerable children.

www.ingramcontent.com/pod-product-compliance
Lightning Source LLC
Chambersburg PA
CBHW071159070526
44584CB00019B/2847